# THIRD READER,

WITH EXCERPTS

FROM THE BEST

AMERICAN

AND

ENGLISH WRITERS

**BY WILLIAM H. McGUFFEY**
**Professor in Miami University,**

Editions 1836 – 1853

CINCINNATI:
PUBLISHED BY TRUMAN AND
150 MAIN STREET

# ROMAN NUMERALS EXPLAINED

A numeral is a symbol meaning number. Our system of counting is believed to have begun by people counting on their fingers. Both the Arabic (1, 2, 3, 4, etc.) and the Roman (I, II, III, IV, etc.) are believed to have started this way. The word digit, meaning number, is from the Latin word digitus, meaning finger. The number V (5) seems to be representative of an open hand; the number X (10) seems to be like two open hands.

In earlier days, our forefathers used the Roman system to indicate chapter headings in books. To help you understand those numbers more easily you may refer to the chart below:

| Roman | Arabic | Roman | Arabic | Roman | Arabic |
|-------|--------|-------|--------|-------|--------|
| I | 1 | XI | 11 | XXX | 30 |
| II | 2 | XII | 12 | XL | 40 |
| III | 3 | XIII | 13 | L | 50 |
| IV | 4 | XIV | 14 | LX | 60 |
| V | 5 | XV | 15 | LXX | 70 |
| VI | 6 | XVI | 16 | LXXX | 80 |
| VII | 7 | XVII | 17 | XC | 90 |
| VIII | 8 | XVIII | 18 | C | 100 |
| IX | 9 | XIX | 19 | D | 500 |
| X | 10 | XX | 20 | M | 1000 |

Entered according to Act of Congress, in the year 1836
By TRUMAN & SMITH,
In the Clerk's Office for the District Court of Ohio.

The Moore–McGuffey Reader_TM is a trademark of Hewitt Research, Inc.

This edition copyright © 1983 by Moore Learning Systems, Box 9, Washougal, Washington 98671

Editors:  Raymond S. Moore
          Dorothy N. Moore
          Jane Thayer

Cover illustration by Greg Constantine

ISBN 0-913717-03-7
Printed in the United States of America

# PREFACE TO THE THIRD READER

When the McGuffey READERS were first published, *eclectic* was a fashionable word in the field of education. Then, as now, competing educational philosophies claimed superiority for their own methods and goals. By using the term *eclectic* in a title, an author or publisher was suggesting that he had gleaned the best from every available philosophy or method. Winthrop B. Smith and Company, one of McGuffey's early publishers, advertised an entire ECLECTIC EDUCATIONAL SERIES including grammar, arithmetic and algebra, as well as the McGuffey READERS.

William McGuffey's use of the word *eclectic* carried a double significance. Besides meaning "built on the best features of all educational philosophies," it also meant that his literary selections were the best pieces taken from many sources.

In the THIRD READER McGuffey continues his emphasis on lessons designed to build character. Although this present THIRD READER contains few lessons that are completely lectures on behavior, nearly all the adventure stories, historical reports, Biblical excerpts, nature articles and poetry include instruction and admonition to encourage a child in personal piety, social responsibility, patriotism and industriousness.

The Biblical selections of the THIRD READER are primarily from the poetry of the Old Testament—Psalms and Isaiah—and from the words of Jesus in the New Testament—the Sermon on the Mount. As late as 1840 the Bible was read daily in all the schools of the West. Although parents did not want sectarian teaching in the schools, "religious instruction was desired by the great majority of school patrons," according to McGuffey editor and historian Henry H. Vail.

In a world without television and colored book illustrations, McGuffey considered it necessary to include detailed descriptions of the insects, animals and other natural wonders presented in the lessons. But nature is not presented merely for scientific investigation. According to McGuffey authority John Westerhoff III, the nature lessons "focus upon the role nature plays in helping us understand God and his ways."

Each of the lessons in the THIRD READER is prefaced with a Rule for Reading. In the era of the great American orators, whose influence stretched even to the little one-room schoolhouses dotting the countryside of the frontier West, classroom instruction emphasized oral reading and elocution.

Questions and a Spell-and-Define word list follow each lesson. All new questions, intended to aid oral discussion or to provide written assignments, were written from the understanding and viewpoint of today's child. The Spell-and-Define list suggests words for spelling and vocabulary development. The numbers before each word refer to the paragraph or stanza where it is found.

—The Publishers

# SUGGESTIONS TO TEACHERS

It is recommended that the pupil be required to *master* everything as he goes along.

The Rules for Reading need not, as a general thing, be memorized, but only well studied, so as to be understood.

The Definitions ought to be made out by the exercise of the pupil's own judgment (aided by the instructor) from the sense which the *connection requires:* for, to seek out and memorize definitions from a dictionary or defining vocabulary only, is injurious rather than beneficial. It is a mere exercise of memory, and nothing else. . . .

The plan of teaching the pupil to *spell*, in conjunction with the exercises in reading, will, it is believed, be found eminently beneficial in fixing in the memory the *orthographical form of words*, not only as they appear in the columns of a spelling book or dictionary, but in all the variety of their different numbers, oblique cases, degrees of comparison, moods, tenses, etc.—while the exercise of *defining* produces a similar effect in regard to the *meaning* of the terms employed; since the learner is required to find out the meaning of each term defined, from the *connection*, without having recourse to an expositor.

It is the *connection alone*, that can convey to the mind the true meaning of words. No two words in any language are exactly alike in signification. How then can definition, *merely*, be made to convey their import?

The Rules given at the beginning of each lesson, designed to assist the learner in acquiring correct habits of reading, are generally short and simple, and have a direct, though not an *exclusive* reference to the lesson which immediately follows. . . .

The questions appended to each lesson are, as in the preceding volume, designed to *suggest* rather than to *direct* the *interrogative* method of oral instruction. The teacher will frequently find questions, the answers to which are not contained in the antecedent lesson, but only suggested by it. This is calculated to awaken inquiry, on the part of the pupil, and to lay the instructor under a kind of obligation to read the lesson over carefully before

he attempts to hear it recited by the learner—a plan
which the author cannot too earnestly recommend in regard to *every possible kind of teaching*.

It is not unusual to give directions to pupils, in connection with those given to teachers.

This appears rather officious. The Teacher, it is pre-
sumed, will be fully competent to the task, and he who
has judgment enough to select for his scholars the best
books, will surely not fail in pointing out to them the best
methods of using them.

—From the 1838 Edition

# CONTENTS

# LESSON I (1)

## *Effects of Rashness*
### S. G. GOODRICH

RULE—To read is to convey by means of the voice to the ear of others, certain thoughts and feelings, which are expressed by letters to the eye.

A certain Persian of distinction had for years been extremely anxious that he might have a son to inherit his estate. His wishes were at length gratified. A son was born, and the fond father was so anxious for the health and safety of the little stranger that he would scarcely suffer it to be taken out of his sight and was never so much delighted as when he was employed in holding it.

One day his wife, on going to the bath, committed the infant to her husband's care, earnestly entreating him not to leave the cradle until she came back. Scarcely, however, had she left the house when the king sent for her husband. To refuse, or to delay obeying the royal summons, was impossible; he, therefore, went immediately to the palace, entrusting the child to the care of a favorite dog which had been bred in the family.

No sooner was the father out of sight than a large snake made its appearance and was crawling towards the cradle. When the dog saw the child's life in danger, he instantly seized the snake by the back of the head and destroyed it.

Soon after, the father returned from court, and the dog, as if conscious of the service he had performed, ran out to meet him. The man saw the dog stained with blood and imagined that he had killed the child. Without making any further reflection or inquiry, he struck the faithful little animal such a blow with his stick, that the dog instantly died.

When the father came into the house, saw the child safe, and the snake lying dead by the side of the cradle, he smote his breast with grief, accusing himself of rashness and ingratitude towards the dog. While he was uttering these woeful lamentations, in came his wife, who, having learned the cause of his distress, blamed him severely for his lack of reflection. He confessed his indiscretion, but begged her not to add reproaches to his distress, since reproof could now avail nothing.

"True," said she, "advice can be of no service in the present instance, but I wish to rouse your mind to reflection that you may reap instruction from your misfortunes. Shame and repentance are the sure consequences of instant anger and lack of reflection."

• • •

The king of Persia once had a favorite hawk. Being one day on a hunting party with his hawk on his hand, a deer started up before him. He let the hawk fly and followed the deer with great eagerness until, at length, it was taken. The courtiers were all left behind in the chase.

The king, being thirsty, rode about in search of water. At last reaching the foot of a mountain, he discovered a little water trickling in drops from the rock. He accordingly took a little cup out of his quiver and held it to catch the water.

Just when the cup was filled, and the king was going to drink, the hawk, which had followed his master, alighted, shook his pinions, and overset the cup. The king was vexed at the accident and again applied the vessel to the hole in the rock. When the cup was replenished and he was lifting it to his mouth, the hawk clapped his wings and again threw it down. At this the king was so enraged that he flung the bird with such force against the ground that it immediately died.

4 At this time one of the king's officers came up. He took a napkin out of a small pouch, wiped the cup, and was going to give the king some water to drink. The king said he had a great inclination to taste the pure water that distilled through the rock, but not having patience to wait for its being collected in drops, he ordered the officer to go to the top of the mountain and fill the cup at the fountain head.

5 The officer, having reached the top of the mountain, saw a large serpent lying dead at the spring and perceived that the poisonous foam of the reptile had mixed with the water which fell in drops through the rock. He descended, related the fact to the king, and presented him with a cup of cold water out of his flagon.

6 When the king lifted the cup to his lips, the tears gushed from his eyes. He then related to the officer the adventure of the hawk and made many reflections upon the destructive consequences of anger and thoughtlessness. During his whole life his breast rankled with sorrow and regret that he had been guilty of such rashness.

QUESTIONS — 1. What character flaw did both of the men in the two stories of this lesson have in common? 2. How should the Persian gentleman have reacted when he saw the blood stains on his dog? 3. How long did the king regret his rash act?

SPELL AND DEFINE — (1) Persian; (2) summons; (4) court; (5) lamentations; (6) reflection; (7) courtiers; (9) pinions; (10) napkin, pouch; (12) consequences.

# LESSON II (2)

## Conflagration of an Amphitheater
### CROLY

RULE—Do not make all parts of a sentence equally emphatic. This often destroys the sense and makes your reading monotonous.

Rome was an ocean of flame. Height and depth were covered with red surges that rolled before the blast like an endless tide. The billows burst up the sides of the hills, which they turned into instant volcanoes, exploding volumes of smoke and fire, then plunged into the depths in a hundred glowing cataracts, then climbed and consumed again.

The distant sound of the city in her convulsion went to the soul. The air was filled with the steady roar of the advancing flame, the crash of falling houses, and the hideous outcry of the myriads flying through the streets or surrounded and perishing in the conflagration.

All was clamor, violent struggle, and helpless death. Men and women of the highest rank were on foot, trampled by the rabble that had then lost all respect of condition. One dense mass of miserable life, irresistible from its weight, crushed by the narrow streets and scorched by the flames over their heads, rolled through the gates like an endless stream of black lava.

The fire had originally broken out upon the Palatine, and hot smoke that wrapped and half blinded us hung thick as night upon the wrecks of pavilions and palaces, but the dexterity and knowledge of my inexplicable guide carried us on.

It was in vain that I insisted upon knowing the

purpose of this terrible traverse. He pressed his
hand on his heart in reassurance of his fidelity and
still spurred on. We now passed under the shade of
an immense range of lofty buildings, whose gloomy
and solid strength seemed to bid defiance to chance
and time.

A sudden yell appalled me. A ring of fire swept
round its summit: burning cordage, sheets of can-
vas, and a shower of all things combustible, flew
into the air above our heads. An uproar followed,
unlike all that I had ever heard, a hideous mixture
of howls, shrieks, and groans.

The flames rolled down the narrow street before
us and made the passage next to impossible. While
we hesitated, a huge fragment of the building
heaved as if in an earthquake and, fortunately for
us, fell inwards. The whole scene of terror was then
open.

The great amphitheater of Statilius Taurus had
caught fire; the stage with its inflammable furniture
was intensely blazing below. The flames were wheel-
ing up, circle above circle, through the seventy
thousand seats that rose from the ground to the
roof. I stood in unspeakable awe and wonder on the
side of this colossal cavern, this mighty temple of
the city of fire. At length a descending blast cleared
away the smoke that covered the arena.

The cause of those horrid cries was now visible.
The wild beasts kept for the games had broken from
their dens. Maddened by fright and pain, lions,
tigers, panthers, wolves, whole herds of the mon-
sters of India and Africa, were enclosed in an im-
passable barrier of fire.

They bounded, they fought, they screamed, they
tore; they ran howling round and round the circle;
they made desperate leaps upwards through the
blaze; they were flung back, and fell only to fasten

their fangs in each other and, with their parching jaws bathed in blood, to die raging.

I looked anxiously to see whether any human being was involved in this fearful catastrophe. To my great relief, I could see none. The keepers and attendants had obviously escaped. As I expressed my gladness, I was startled by a loud cry from my guide, the first sound that I had heard him utter.

He pointed to the opposite side of the amphitheater. There indeed sat an object of melancholy interest—a man who had been either unable to escape or had determined to die. Escape was now impossible. He sat in desperate calmness on his funeral pile. He was a gigantic Ethiopian slave, entirely naked.

He had chosen his place, as if in mockery, on the imperial throne; the fire was above him and around him, and under this tremendous canopy. He gazed, without the movement of a muscle, on the combat of the wild beasts below. He was a solitary sovereign, with the whole tremendous game played for himself and inaccessible to the power of man.

QUESTIONS — 1. How can you tell that this is an eyewitness account? 2. The fire started on the Palatine. Using an encyclopedia, find out what the Palatine is. 3. Describe the scene in the amphitheater.

SPELL AND DEFINE — (1) surges, volumes, cataracts; (2) myriads; (4) dexterity; (6) combustible; (7) earthquake; (8) amphitheater, arena; (11) catastrophe.

# LESSON III (3)

## *Advantages of Industry*—ABBOTT

RULE—There are certain positions of the body in which it is un-healthy to read or speak. Ease in pronouncing requires that you should stand or sit erect, holding the head up and throwing the shoulders back.

Charles did not possess superior talents, but he was a good student. When quite young, he was always careful and diligent in school. Sometimes, when there was a *very hard* lesson, instead of going out to play during recess, he would stay in to study. He had resolved that his first object should be to get his lessons well, and then he could play with a good conscience. He loved to play as well as anybody and was one of the best players on the playground. I hardly ever saw any boy catch a ball better than he could. When playing any game, everyone was glad to get Charles on his side.

I have said that Charles would sometimes stay in at recess. This, however, was very seldom; it was only when the lesson was very hard indeed. Generally he was among the first on the playground, and he was also among the first to go into school, when called. Hard study gave him a relish for play, and play again gave him a relish for hard study. So he was happy both in school and out. The principal could not help liking him, for he always had his lessons well committed and never gave him any trouble.

When he went to enter college, the principal gave him a good recommendation. He was able to answer all the questions which were put to him when he was examined. He had studied so well when he was in high school, and was so thoroughly prepared for college, that he found it very easy to keep up with his class. And he had much time for reading interesting books.

But he would always get his lesson well before he did anything else and would review it just before class. When called upon to answer a question, he rose tranquil and happy and very seldom made mistakes. The officers of the college had a high opinion of him, and he was respected by all the students.

There was in the college a society made up of all the best scholars. Charles was chosen a member of that society. It was the custom to choose someone of the society to deliver a public address every year. This honor was conferred on Charles. And he had studied so diligently and read so much, that he delivered an address which was very interesting to all who heard it.

At last he graduated and received his degree. It was known by all that he was a good scholar, and by all that he was respected. His father and mother, brothers and sisters, came on the commencement day to hear him speak.

They all felt gratified and loved Charles more than ever. Many situations of usefulness and profit were opened to him, for Charles was now an intelligent man and universally respected. He is still a useful and a happy man. He has a cheerful home and is esteemed by all who know him.

Such are the rewards of industry. How strange it is that any person should be willing to live in idleness, when it will certainly make them unhappy! The idle child is almost invariably poor and miserable; the industrious child is happy and prosperous.

But perhaps some child who reads this, asks, "Does God notice little children in school?" He certainly does. You are placed in this world to improve your time. In youth you must be preparing for future usefulness.

"With books, or work, or healthful play,
   Let your first years be past,
That you may give, for every day,
   Some good account at last."

QUESTIONS — 1. If Charles did not possess superior talents, why was he able to make superior achievements? 2. Consider your work, study, and play habits. Are they designed to produce the kind of adult you want to be?

SPELL AND DEFINE — (1) superior, conscience; (3) recommendation; (4) tranquil, opinion; (5) society, conferred; (6) scholar, commencement; (7) esteemed.

# LESSON IV (4)

## *How a Fly Walks on the Ceiling*—PEARL

RULE—Endeavor always to adapt your mode of reading to the nature and style of that which you read. Grave, lighthearted, tender and sublime subjects have each a general style of reading which is peculiarly suited to them.

"Papa, will you explain to us the means by which flies are enabled to ascend a pane of glass and walk with ease along the ceiling of the room? You know you told us the other day you would so."

"Well, Harriet, I will try, though I am not sure that I shall be able to make you understand me."

"Oh, never fear that," exclaimed Harriet and her two little brothers at the same time. "We can surely understand how a fly walks. It must be very simple."

"Undoubtedly very simple, but it requires some previous knowledge of science."

"Oh, if the walking of a fly or mosquito is at all connected with science, I assure you I shall want to know nothing about it, for I hate science. It is such dry stuff."

"Papa, never mind my sister," said William. "James and I want very much to understand, and Harriet need not stay to hear the explanation if she does not wish to."

"Well, my boys, come to the library. I have just arranged my solar microscope to show you the foot and leg of a fly, and some other curious things. I have likewise my air pump ready, which will help to explain what you want to know."

Harriet looked a little disappointed and wished that she had not pronounced so decidedly against science, for she was very fond of seeing and only disliked the labor of studying. Her papa, observing the moody expression of her lively countenance, said, "I wish you, William, to try and persuade your sister to overcome so much of her dislike of science, for the present, as to accompany us to the library." William had no difficult task to perform, and in a minute they were all seated in the library eager to hear all that could be said about the little pedestrian.

The father began, "My children, the fly, every time he moves his foot, performs a scientific feat, similar in every respect, to that which I now show you by moving the handle of the air pump. You perceive that this glass vessel which is put on this brass plate, now adheres so firmly to it, that I am unable to force it away."

"How is this done, Father? It looks like some conjuror's trick. I see nothing pressing upon the glass to cause it to stick so fast."

"Though you cannot see it, I assure you there is

something pressing very hard all around it, and that is the air."

"You astonish me. Has the air weight? I never heard of that before. I shall never say again, 'as light as air.' "

"But you have heard of hurricanes sweeping away forests and houses, and rendering the countries over which they passed, a wilderness. And in truth, they are almost as much to be dreaded as earthquakes, and a hurricane is only air put in motion."

"I have been very stupid not to find out that air has weight. But how is it that we do not feel it, Papa?" continued Harriet.

"I have had a more puzzling question to answer, I assure you. The air is a very subtle fluid and finds its way into every crevice. One of its properties is, that it presses equally in all directions, up and down, and sideways, with equal force. We only perceive its weight when we remove the air from one side of a body, so as to cause the whole weight to be upon the other. From this glass vessel I withdrew the air that was in the inside of it, and which pressed it upwards with a force exactly equal to that with which the air above pressed downwards, and then the whole weight of the atmosphere pressing in one direction kept it firmly attached to the brass plate."

"That is a very beautiful arrangement," cried William. "I shall never breathe the air again without thinking of its wonderful properties."

"I will take off this vessel and put this one on, which is open at both ends. Now put your hand, Harriet, on the upper end, and I will cause a slight vacuum to take place so that you may feel the pressure."

"Stop, Father, you will crush my hand to pieces if

you move that handle another time. Do look at my hand, William; the grip of a giant would be nothing to that."

William tried the experiment himself. "How heavy is the atmosphere, Papa? I should like to know that."

"It is very great. It presses upon the surface of all bodies near the level of the ocean with a force equal to fourteen pounds on every square inch.

"I think you can now understand that if a fly has the power to extract the air from its feet as it moves along, the pressure of the atmosphere is sufficient to hold it fast to any surface, however smooth, and however much inclined to the horizon."

"If the fly can do that, he is more of a scientist than I took him to be," said William. "But I am impatient to see how the little fellow accomplishes the feat."

"Here is the leg of a common fly that I have placed in the solar microscope. It is now so much magnified that we can examine the various parts of it with ease."

"What a strange looking thing it is, and so large! My arm is nothing to it. How I should like to see an elephant put into a microscope," said Harriet.

"What an idea, Harriet! Why it would appear as large as one of the Alps," exclaimed William.

"We only use microscopes to examine bodies that are too delicate for the eye, but you will observe that the leg is hollow for there is a line of light running up the middle of it, which you can easily perceive. At the foot you can distinctly observe a flap or membrane, to which are attached two points, one in front, and the other behind. These the fly can move at pleasure and can extend or contract the flap just as it pleases.

"When Mr. Fly then wishes to pay a visit of ceremony to a distinguished acquaintance or to move with gravity around his fair one without the trouble of raising himself in the air, he stretches out these points, tightens the flap, draws the air from under it, and moves along the polished surface of the glass with as much ease and security as you can on the broad gravel walk in the garden."

"How delightful! How beautiful! How ingenious!" they all exclaimed at once. "I shall never see a fly again without interest."

QUESTIONS — 1. What features of a fly's legs make it possible for it to walk on the ceiling? 2. Give examples that demonstrate that air has weight.

SPELL AND DEFINE — (1) ceiling; (6) explanation; (7) microscope; (8) observing; (13) hurricane; (15) crevice; (16) vacuum; (20) horizon; (26) distinguished; (27) ingenious.

# LESSON V (5)

## *Select Sentences and Paragraphs*

RULE—In reading short sentences, such as the following, be careful to place the emphasis upon the right word.

1. Innocence is better than repentance.

2. If you behave better in one place than in another, let that place be home.

3. To say little and perform much is the characteristic of a great mind.

4. Neglect no opportunity of doing good.

5. Modesty is one of the chief ornaments of youth.

6. No confidence can be placed in those who are in the habit of lying.

7. Our reputation, virtue and happiness greatly depend on the choice of our companions.

8. Good or bad habits, formed in youth, generally go with us through life.

9. Never sport with pain and distress, in any of your amusements, nor treat even the meanest insect with wanton cruelty.

10. It should be a general rule never to utter anything in conversation which would justly dishonor us if it should be reported to the world.

11. The acquisition of knowledge is one of the most honorable occupations of youth.

12. Our best friends are those who tell us of our faults and teach us how to correct them.

13. Vice, sooner or later, brings misery. Deceit is the mark of a little mind. Cultivate a love of truth. Think before you speak, and deliberate before you promise.

14. We should be kind to all persons, even to those who are unkind to us. We can never treat a fellow creature ill without offending the gracious Creator and Father of all.

15. They who ridicule the wise and good are dangerous companions; they poison the judgment and bring virtue itself into contempt.

16. Gratitude is a delightful emotion. The grateful heart performs its duty at the same time that it endears itself to others.

17. Ingratitude is a crime so shameful that the man was never yet found who would acknowledge himself guilty of it.

18. Pride and self-sufficiency stifle sentiments of dependence on our Creator; levity and attachment to worldly pleasures destroy the sense of gratitude to Him.

19. By taking revenge, a man is but even with his enemy, but in passing over an injury, he is superior. No revenge is so truly heroic as doing good in return for evil.

20. If the spring put forth no blossom, in summer there will be no beauty and in autumn no fruit. So, if youth be trifled away in idleness and misapplication, manhood will be contemptible, and old age wretched. Death is terrible to those whose life has passed away without love to God and benefit to man.

QUESTION — Choose one of these proverbs, write it neatly at the top of a page of paper, and then write a story that illustrates the truth of the proverb.

SPELL AND DEFINE — (1) innocence; (7) reputation; (13) deceit, deliberate; (16) gratitude; (18) stifle; (20) contemptible.

# LESSON VI (6)

## *Alexander the Great*

RULE—Emphasis belongs both to words and to whole clauses of sentences. Sometimes in order to bring out fully the meaning of a passage, it is necessary to give emphasis to several successive words or to a considerable part of the whole sentence.

Macedon was, for a long time, a small state in Greece, not celebrated for anything, except that its kings always governed according to the laws of the country and that their children were well educated.

At length, after many kings had reigned over Macedon, one named Philip came to the throne, who determined to render his kingdom as illustrious as other kingdoms. He raised a large army, subdued many people, and contrived to make the other states of Greece quarrel among themselves.

When they were quite tired with fighting against each other, he induced them all to submit to him, which they were the more ready to do because he gave them hopes that he would lead them on to conquer Persia. But before he set out on his expedition to Persia, he was killed by one of his own subjects.

Philip was succeeded by his son Alexander, called in history, "Alexander the Great." On Philip's death, the Greeks thought themselves at liberty and resolved that Macedon should no longer hold them in subjection, but Alexander quickly showed them that he was as politically wise as his father and still bolder than he.

Alexander caused his father's murderers to be put to death, and then collecting his army, in an assembly of the Grecian states he delivered a speech, which convinced them of his wisdom and valor. After this they agreed to make him, as his father had been, chief commander of Greece. He then returned to Macedon, and in a short time afterwards began his conquests, gaining surprising victories and obliging all who fought against him to submit.

As soon as Alexander had settled the Grecian states to his wishes, he crossed the Hellespont, (now called the Dardanelles) with his army, in order to subdue Persia. The Persians, hearing of this, assembled their forces and waited for him on the banks of the river called the Granicus. When the Grecians arrived on the opposite side, one of the generals advised Alexander to let his soldiers rest a little, but he was so eager for conquest that he gave command instantly to march through the Granicus.

His troops, having found a shallow place, obeyed. The trumpets sounded and loud shouts of joy were heard throughout the army. As soon as the Persians saw them advancing, they let fly showers of arrows at them, and when they were going to land, strove to push them back into the water—but in vain; Alexander and his army landed and a dreadful battle was fought, in which he proved victorious. He then, advancing from city to city, obliged them to own him for their king instead of Darius.

Darius, being informed of Alexander's progress, resolved to meet him with a great army. As soon as Alexander heard of his approach, he prepared to encounter him at Issus, where he obliged him to flee, leaving behind him his queen and family and immense treasure, all of which Alexander seized.

Some time afterwards, Darius fought another battle at Arbela, in which he was again defeated. Soon after this he was killed, and thus ended the Persian Empire.

Not contented with the conquest of Persia, Alexander resolved to subdue the kings of India and he obliged many of them to submit. One of them, named Porus, resisted him with great courage, but Alexander overcame him at last. He treated him, however, with much respect, gave him his liberty and restored him to his kingdom. Porus proved a faithful friend to him ever afterwards.

Between the battles which Alexander fought with Darius, he subdued many states and kingdoms, and among others, Egypt and Babylon. After the death of Darius, he made still further conquests, besides those of the Indian princes, by which means the Grecian empire was raised to a great height.

When Alexander rested from fighting, he took up his residence at Babylon and lived there in the utmost splendor. But his glory was of short duration, for he had one very great fault, which was that of being excessively fond of eating and drinking. He wanted to make the world believe that he was a god and could do whatever he chose. When he was at a banquet, he would try to drink more wine than any other man in the company.

At length, he engaged to empty a cup, called Hercules' cup, which held six bottles of wine. And it is said he actually did so. But it proved the cause of his death, the wine heating his blood to such a degree that it brought on a violent fever, which soon put an end to his life. He died three hundred and twenty-three years before the Christian era, at the age of thirty-two.

How shocking it is to think that a man who had subdued so many nations should suffer himself to be conquered by the sin of intemperance. It is a lamentable truth that intemperance kills more than the sword.

The glory of the Grecian empire was terminated by the death of Alexander, for as he had no son fit to reign after him, and did not determine who should be his successor, the principal commanders of his army divided his conquests among themselves, and after many quarrels and battles, that which was one empire under Alexander became four separate kingdoms.

QUESTIONS — 1. What occurred that caused Alexander to become ruler of Greece at the early age of 20? 2. What kingdoms did he conquer? 3. What was Alexander's great fault?

SPELL AND DEFINE — (5) conquest; (6) Hellespont, Dardanelles, Granicus; (8) encounter; (12) banquet; (14) intemperance.

# LESSON VII (7)

## *The Child's Inquiry*

RULE—Remember that in reading poetry there is always some danger of forgetting the sense in the rhyme, and therefore of reading, not as if you were expressing some thought or feeling to another mind, but as if you were chanting something to please the ear.

Son:      How big was Alexander, Pa,
          That people call him great?
      Was he, like old Goliath, tall—
          His spear an hundred weight?
      Was he so large that he could stand
          Like some tall steeple high;
      And while his feet were on the ground,
          His hands could touch the sky?

Father:  O no, my child: about as large
          As I or Uncle James.
      'Twas not his *stature* made him great,
          But greatness of his *name*.

Son:      His *name* so great? I know 'tis *long*,
          But easy quite to spell—
      And more than half a year ago
          I knew it very well.

Father:  I mean, my child, his *actions* were
          So great, he got a name,
      That everybody speaks with praise,
          That tells about his fame.

Son:      Well, what great actions did he do?
          I want to know it all.

Father:  Why, he it was that conquered Tyre,
          And leveled down her wall:

And thousands of her people slew—
   And then to Persia went—
And fire and sword on every side
   Through many a region sent.
A hundred conquered cities shone
   With midnight burnings red—
And, strewed o'er many a battle ground
   A thousand soldiers bled.

Son:     Did *killing people* make him great?
   Then why was Abdel Young,
Who killed his neighbor, training day,
   Put into jail and hung?
I never heard them call him great.

Father: Why, no—'twas not in war—
   And him that kills a single man,
His neighbors all abhor.

Son:     Well then, if I should kill a man,
   I'd kill a HUNDRED more;
I *should* be GREAT, and not get hung
   Like Abdel Young, before.

Father: Not so, my child. 'Twill never do:—
   The Gospel bids be kind.

Son:     Then they that *kill* and they that *praise*
   The Gospel do not mind.

Father: You know, my child, the Bible says,
   That you must always do
To other people, as you wish
   To have them do to you.

Son:     But, Pa, did Alexander wish
   That some strong man would come
And burn his house, and kill him too,
   And do as he had done?
And everybody calls him GREAT
   For killing people so!

Well, now, what *right* he had to kill,
  I should be glad to know.
If one should burn the buildings here,
  And kill the folks within—
Would anybody call him great,
  For such a wicked thing?

QUESTIONS — 1. This poem presents a contradiction in values: Why should Abdel Young, who killed one man, be punished by hanging, while Alexander, who was responsible for the deaths of thousands, be praised and called, "Great"? What causes this contradiction? 2. Do you think Alexander deserves to be called "Great"? Explain your answer.

SPELL AND DEFINE — (2) stature; (6) conquered; (10) gospel.

# LESSON VIII (8)

## *A Contest with Tigers*

RULE—Never neglect to pronounce the little words distinctly because they are little. Much sometimes depends upon them.

On leaving the Indian village, we continued to wind around Chimborazo's wide base. A dense fog was now gathering around it, and its snow-covered head was hidden from our view. Our guides looked anxiously about and announced their apprehension of a violent storm.

We soon found that their fears were well founded. The thunder began to roll and resounded through the mountainous passes with the most terrific grandeur. Then came the vivid lightning: flash following flash—above, around, beneath—everywhere a sea of fire.

We sought a momentary shelter in a cleft of the rocks while one of our Indian guides hastened forward to seek a more secure asylum. In a short time he returned and informed us that he had discovered a spacious cavern which would afford us sufficient protection from the storm. We proceeded there immediately, and with great difficulty and not a little danger, we at last got into it.

When the storm had somewhat abated, our guide ventured out, in order to ascertain if it were possible to continue our journey. The cave in which we had taken refuge was so extremely dark that if we moved a few paces from the entrance, we could hardly see an inch before us. We were debating as to the propriety of leaving it, even before the Indians came back, when we suddenly heard a singular groaning or growling in the farther end of the cavern, which instantly fixed all our attention.

Wharton and myself listened anxiously, but our daring and inconsiderate young friend Lincoln, together with my huntsman, crept about upon their hands and knees and endeavored to discover by groping, from whence the sound proceeded.

They had not advanced far into the cavern, before we heard them utter an exclamation of surprise—and they returned to us, each carrying in his arms an animal singularly marked and about the size of a cat, seemingly of great strength and power, and furnished with immense fangs. The eyes were of a green color, strong claws were upon their feet, and a blood-red tongue hung out of their mouths.

Wharton had scarcely glanced at them, when he exclaimed in consternation, "We have come into the den of a—" He was interrupted by a fearful cry of dismay from our guides, who came rushing precipitately towards us, calling out, "A tiger! A tiger!" and at the same with extraordinary rapidity, they climbed up a cedar tree, which stood at the entrance of the cave and hid themselves among the branches.

Wharton called us to assist him instantly in blocking up the mouth of the cave with an immense stone which fortunately lay near it. The sense of approaching danger augmented our strength—for we now distinctly heard the growl of the ferocious animal, and we were lost beyond redemption if he reached the entrance before we could get it closed.

Before this was done, we could distinctly see the tiger bounding towards the spot and stooping in order to creep into his den by the narrow opening. At this fearful moment our exertions were successful, and the great stone kept the wild beast at bay.

There was a small open space, however, between the top of the entrance and the stone, through which we could see the head of the animal, illuminated by his glowing eyes, which he rolled glaring with fury upon us. His frightful roaring penetrated to the depths of the cavern and was answered by the hoarse growling of the cubs.

Our ferocious enemy attempted first to remove the stone with his powerful claws and then to push it with his head from its place; and these efforts, proving useless, served only to increase his wrath. He uttered a tremendous heart-piercing howl, and his flaming eyes darted light into the darkness of our retreat.

He went backwards and forwards before the entrance of the cave in the most wild and impetuous manner, then stood still and, stretching out his neck in the direction of the forest, broke forth in a deafening howl.

Our two Indian guides took advantage of this opportunity to discharge several arrows from the tree. He was struck more than once, but the light weapons bounded back harmlessly from his skin. At length, however, one of them struck him near the eye, and the arrow remained sticking in the wound.

He now broke anew into the wildest fury, sprang at the tree and tore it with his claws, as if he would have dragged it to the ground. But having, at length, succeeded in getting rid of the arrow, he became more calm and laid himself down, as before, in front of the cave.

One of our party had strangled the two cubs, and before we were aware of what he intended, he threw them through the opening to the tiger. No sooner did the animal perceive them, than he gazed earnestly upon them and began to examine them closely, turning them cautiously from side to side. As soon as he became aware that they were dead, he uttered so piercing a howl of sorrow, that we were obliged to put our hands to our ears.

The thunder had now ceased, and the storm had sunk to a gentle gale; the songs of birds were again heard in the neighboring forest, and the sunbeams sparkled in the drops that hung from the leaves. We saw, through the aperture, how all nature was reviving after the wild war of elements, which had so recently taken place. But the contrast only made our situation more terrible.

The tiger had laid himself down beside his whelps. He was a beautiful animal of great size and strength, and his limbs being stretched out at their full length displayed his immense power of muscle. A double row of great teeth stood far enough apart to show his large red tongue, from which the white foam fell in great drops.

All at once another roar was heard at a distance, and the tiger immediately rose and answered it with a mournful howl. At the same instant, our Indians uttered a cry which announced that some new danger threatened us. A few moments confirmed our worst fears; for another tiger, not quite so large as the former, came rapidly towards the spot where we were.

The howls which the tigress gave, when she had examined the bodies of her cubs, surpassed everything horrible that we had yet heard; and the tiger mingled his mournful cries with hers. Suddenly her roaring was lowered to a hoarse growling, and we saw her anxiously stretch out her head, extend her wide and smoking nostrils, and look as if she were determined to discover immediately the murderers of her young.

Her eyes quickly fell upon us, and she made a spring forward with the intention of penetrating to our place of refuge. Perhaps she might have been enabled by her immense strength to push away the stone had we not, with all our united power, held it against her.

When she found that all her efforts were fruitless, she approached the tiger, who lay stretched out beside his cubs, and he rose and joined in her hollow roarings. They stood together for a few moments, as if in consultation, then suddenly went off at a rapid pace and disappeared from our sight. Their howling died away in the distance, and then entirely ceased.

Our Indians descended from their tree, and urged us to seize the only possibility of our yet saving ourselves—by instant flight; for the tigers had only gone round the height to seek another inlet to the cave, with which they were, no doubt, well acquainted. In the greatest haste the stone was pushed aside, and we stepped forth from what we had considered a living grave.

QUESTIONS — 1. Did the men set out on a tiger hunt? 2. What did the tiger and tigress do that showed they had strong feelings for their cubs? 3. Do you think it was necessary for the men to kill the cubs? Explain your answer.

SPELL AND DEFINE — (2) resounded, terrific; (3) momentary, asylum; (4) abated; (5) inconsiderate; (6) exclamation; (7) precipitately; (8) augmented; (10) illuminated; (12) impetuous; (19) hoarse.

# LESSON IX (9)

## *The Thunderstorm*—MRS. HEMANS

RULE—In reading poetry, keep your eyes to the punctuation, as that will guide you often to the sense and enable you to avoid the habit of dropping the voice uniformly at the end of a line.

Deep, fiery clouds o'erspread the sky,
  Dead stillness reigns in air;
There is not even a breeze, on high,
  The gossamer to bear.

The woods are hushed, the waters rest,
  The lake is dark and still,
Reflecting, on its shadowy breast,
  Each form of rock and hill.

The lime-leaf waves not in the grove,
  Nor rose-tree in the bower;
The birds have ceased their songs of love,
  Aw'd by the threat'ning hour.

'Tis noon; yet nature's calm profound
  Seems as at midnight deep;
But, hark! what peal of awful sound
  Breaks on creation's sleep?

The thunder bursts! Its rolling might
  Seems the firm hills to shake;

And, in terrific splendor bright,
  The gathering lightnings break.

Yet fear not, shrink not thou, my child!
  Though, by the bolt's descent,
Were the tall cliffs in ruins piled,
  And the wide forests rent.

Doth not thy God behold thee still,
  With all-surveying eye?
Doth not his power all nature fill,
  Around, beneath, on high?

Know, hadst thou eagle-pinions, free
  To track the realms of air,
Thou couldst not reach a spot where He
  Would not be with thee there.

In the wide city's peopled towers,
  On the vast ocean's plains,
'Midst the deep woodland's loneliest bowers,
  Alike, the Almighty reigns!

QUESTIONS — According to this poem, what knowledge should comfort you in the midst of a thunderstorm?

SPELL AND DEFINE — (1) gossamer; (2) reflecting; (3) threatening; (4) profound; (5) terrific; (7) all-surveying; (8) loneliest.

# LESSON X (10)

## *The Skylark*—MRS. HEMANS

RULE—In ordinary poetry, do not let the voice fall at the end of
the line, unless there is a point. Nothing is more incorrect than
to pause *uniformly* at the end of every line.

> The Skylark, when the dews of morn
> Hang tremulous on flower and thorn,
> And violets round his nest exhale
> Their fragrance, on the early gale,
> To the first sunbeam spreads his wings,
> Buoyant with joy, and soars, and sings.
>
> He rests not on the leafy spray,
> To warble his exulting lay,
> But high above the morning cloud
> Mounts in triumphant freedom proud;
> And swells, when nearest to the sky,
> His sweetest notes of ecstasy.
>
> Thus, my Creator! thus the more
> My spirit's wing to Thee can soar,
> The more she triumphs to behold
> Thy love in all Thy works unfold;
> And bids her hymns of rapture be
> Most glad, when rising most to Thee.

QUESTION — What does the skylark teach the poetess about
her own experience with her Creator?

SPELL AND DEFINE — (1) tremulous, fragrance; (2) trium-
phant, ecstasy; (3) rapture.

# LESSON XI (11)

## *Murderer's Creek*—PAULDING

RULE—In learning to read, be not in too much haste to get onward, but read deliberately, and yet without drawing out your
words.

Little more than a century ago, the beautiful
region watered by Murderer's Creek was possessed
by a small tribe of Indians, who have long since
become extinct or incorporated with some other
tribe of the West. Three or four hundred yards from
the stream, a white family of the name of Stacy had
established itself in a log house, by tacit permission
of the tribe to whom Stacy had made himself useful
by his skill in a variety of little arts highly estimated by the Indians.

In particular, a friendship developed between him
and an old Indian called Naoman, who often came to
his house and partook of his hospitality. The
Indians seldom forgive injuries or forget benefits.
The family consisted of Stacy, his wife, and two children, a boy and a girl, the former five, the latter
three years old.

One day Naoman came to Stacy's log hut and, in
his absence, lighted his pipe and sat down. He
looked very serious, sometimes sighed deeply, but
said not a word. Stacy's wife asked him what was
the matter? Was he sick? He shook his head, sighed,
but said nothing and soon went away.

The next day he came again and behaved in the
same manner. Stacy's wife began to think strange
of this and related it to her husband, who advised
her to urge the old man to an explanation the next
time he came. Accordingly, when he repeated his

visit the day after, she was more insistent than usual.

At last the old Indian said, "I am a red man and the pale faces are our enemies. Why should I speak?"

"But my husband and I are your friends. You have eaten salt with us a thousand times, and my children have sat on your knee as often. If you have anything on your mind, tell it to me."

"It will cost me my life, if it is known, and the white-faced women are not good at keeping secrets," replied Naoman.

"Try me and see."

"Will you swear, by your Great Spirit, that you will tell none but your husband?"

"I have none else to tell."

"But will you swear?"

"I do swear, by our Great Spirit, that I will tell none but my husband."

"Not if my tribe should kill you for not telling?"

"Not if your tribe should kill me for not telling."

Naoman then proceeded to tell her, that owing to some encroachments of the white people below the mountains, his tribe had become irritated and were resolved, that night, to massacre all the white settlers within their reach; that she must send for her husband, inform him of the danger, and as secretly and speedily as possible, take their canoe and paddle with all haste over the river to Fishkill for safety.

"Be quick, and do nothing that may excite suspicion," said Naoman, as he departed.

The good wife sought her husband, who was down on the river fishing, told him the story and, as no time was to be lost, they proceeded to their boat, which was unluckily filled with water. It took some time to clear it out and, meanwhile, Stacy remembered his gun, which had been left behind. He proceeded to the house and returned with it. All this took up time, and precious time it proved to this poor family.

The daily visits of old Naoman, and his more than ordinary gravity, had excited suspicion in some of the tribe, who had, accordingly, paid particular attention to the movements of Stacy. One of the young Indians, who had been kept on the watch, seeing the whole family about to take to the boat, ran to the little Indian village about a mile off and gave the alarm.

Five Indians collected, ran down to the river, where their canoes were moored, jumped in, and paddled after Stacy, who, by this time, had got some distance out into the stream. They gained on him so fast that twice he dropped his paddle and took up his gun.

But his wife prevented his shooting by telling him that, if he fired and they were afterwards overtaken, they would meet with no mercy from the Indians. He accordingly refrained and plied his paddle till the sweat rolled in big drops down his forehead. All would not do; they were overtaken within a hundred yards of the shore and carried back with shouts and yells of triumph.

When they came on shore, the Indians set fire to Stacy's house and dragged himself, his wife, and children to their village. Here the principal old men, with Naoman among them, assembled to deliberate on the affair.

The chief men of the council stated that some of the tribe had, undoubtedly, been guilty of treason in apprising Stacy and his family of the designs of the tribe, whereby they took the alarm and well nigh escaped. He proposed to examine the prisoners to learn who gave the information.

The old men assented to this and Naoman among the rest. Stacy was first interrogated by one of the old men who spoke English and interpreted to the others. Stacy refused to betray his informant.

His wife was then questioned, while at the same moment, two Indians stood threatening the two children with tomahawks in case she did not confess. She attempted to evade the truth by declaring she had had a dream the night before, which alarmed her, and that she had persuaded her husband to flee.

"The Great Spirit never deigns to talk in dreams to a white face," said the old Indian. "Woman, thou has two tongues and two faces. Speak the truth or thy children shall surely die." The little boy and girl were then brought close to her, and the two savages stood over them ready to execute their bloody orders.

"Wilt thou name," said the old Indian, "the red man who betrayed his tribe? I will ask thee three times." The mother answered not.

"Wilt thou name the traitor? This is the second time." The poor mother looked at her husband, and then at her children, and stole a glance at Naoman, who sat smoking his pipe with invincible gravity.

She wrung her hands and wept, but remained silent. "Wilt thou name the traitor? 'Tis the third and last time." The agony of the mother waxed more bitter. Again she sought the eye of Naoman, but it was cold and motionless.

A pause of a moment awaited her reply, and the tomahawks were raised over the heads of the children, who besought their mother not to let them be murdered.

"Stop," cried Naoman. All eyes were turned upon him. "Stop," repeated he in a tone of authority. "White woman, thou hast kept thy word with me to the last moment. I am the traitor. I have eaten of the salt, warmed myself at the fire, shared the kindness of these Christian white people, and it was I that told them of their danger.

"I am a withered, leafless, branchless trunk. Cut me down, if you will. I am ready." A yell of indignation sounded on all sides. Naoman descended from the little bank where he sat, shrouded his face with his mantle of skins and submitted to his fate. By a blow of the tomahawk, he fell dead at the feet of the white woman.

But the sacrifice of Naoman and the firmness of the Christian white woman did not suffice to save the lives of the other victims. They perished—how, it is needlesss to say. And the memory of their fate has been preserved in the name of the pleasant stream, on whose banks they lived and died, which, to this day is called Murderer's Creek.

QUESTIONS — 1. This story is a story that illustrates nobility of character. What noble act did the white woman perform? 2. Why did she do it? 3. What noble act did Naoman perform? 4. Why did he do it? 5. Are acts of nobility always justly rewarded?

SPELL AND DEFINE — (1) century, tacit; (18) gravity, suspicion; (20) refrained; (22) apprising; (24) tomahawk; (27) traitor; (28) motionless; (31) shrouded; (32) firmness, preserved.

# LESSON XII (12)

## How to Guard Against Temptation

RULE—In reading long words, do not hurry over the syllables or crowd them together. Let each one be pronounced distinctly.

Do you know what temptation is? I will tell you. Suppose you go to school some morning, determined to do your duty there faithfully. Your playmate, sitting in the next seat, watches a moment when the teacher is engaged and reaches out his hand to give you some nuts, which he has brought to school.

He knows that it is wrong for him to offer them, and you know that it would be wrong for you to receive them at such a time. Still it is very hard for you to study while thus tempted. It would be very unpleasant for you to be apparently so uncivil and ungrateful as to take no notice of your playmate's kind offer.

So far as you are concerned, it would really be a kind offer, but so far as his duties to the school are concerned, it would be wrong. You would be strongly tempted in such a case, to receive them, though the receiving of them would be plainly wrong. It would be a violation of your duty to the school, for you ought to perform your part just as faithfully when the teacher is not looking at you, as when he is.

You see thus, that the strength of temptation to do wrong, depends a great deal upon circumstances. You may be generally desirous of doing your duty, and yet peculiar circumstances may occur which will make it very hard for you to do it. In fact, they may be so varied and so peculiar as to increase the temptation very much indeed.

For instance, in the case already mentioned, of the boy handing you the nuts: suppose, that just as his hand is reached out to you, you should perceive that the teacher is turning around and will see him unless you take the nuts quickly. Here is a new circumstance, and it makes the temptation much greater than it was before.

The boy knows perhaps that you have often taken nuts in school from him, in such a way. He does not know of your resolution to perform all your duties faithfully and of your determination to do nothing which will displease God; so he holds out the nuts and seems very impatient for you to take them. And you see by a glance that unless you do take them quickly, he will be seen, and perhaps punished—punished too, for his kindness to you.

It would be very hard for you to do your duty in such a case when you might save him all the consequences by doing what, after all, would seem not to be very wrong; for most boys would think it would not really be very wrong to take the nuts in such a case.

That would be a very strong temptation, but still the boy who was determined to do just right would resist it. He would firmly do his duty, let the consequences be what they would. His friend might perhaps be detected and punished by having all his nuts taken away, or by being kept at his seat during recess, and then after school, the following dialog might take place.

"Why didn't you take those nuts I offered you, John? Couldn't you see I was reaching them out to you?"

"Yes, I saw, but I did not take them because I thought it would be wrong."

"Wrong! What do you mean by that? What a fool you are!"

"You may call me a fool, if you think best, but I am not going to do such things in school any more. I am going to do, as nearly as I can, what is right, whether the teacher is looking or not. I am very sorry you lost your nuts, for it was very kind of you to offer them to me; and to prove that I am sorry, tomorrow I am going to bring you twice as many as you lost."

Now if a boy should really take that course, his influence and example would be very great in leading the other boys to do right. If he was a boy of noble and generous spirit in other things, he would be the more respected for his firmness here and in the end it would be pleasanter and happier for all, that he did his duty. So it always is with temptation to sin. It is hard to resist at the time, but it is far better, far nobler, to do what is right, however painful it may be. And in the end it will be far happier for all concerned.

QUESTIONS — 1. When should you make your decision to always do right whether or not someone is watching you—before or during a temptation? Why? 2. Name Bible characters who were able to resist temptation because they had decided *before* the temptation to always do what is right.

# LESSON XIII (13)

## *Short Sentences*—JOHN MASON

RULE—*Emphasis* is a very important part of reading. Without it, our reading would be dull and monotonous. Words printed in *italics* should always be emphasized, except in the Bible.

1. It signifies nothing to say we will not change our *religion*, if our religion change not *us*.

2. A desire of happiness is natural, a desire of holiness supernatural.

3. If you forget God when you are young, God may forget you when you are old.

4. It will cost something to be religious; it will cost more not to be so.

5. We may expect God's *protection* so long as we live in God's *bounds*.

6. They who deserve *nothing* should be content with *anything*.

7. A man may be poor in purse, yet proud in spirit.

8. How canst thou be a judge of another's heart, that dost not know thine own?

9. They that do nothing are in the ready way to do that which is worse than nothing.

10. Christian graces are like perfumes; the more they are pressed, the sweeter they smell. They are like stars that shine brightest in the dark; like trees, the more they are shaken, the deeper root they take and the more fruit they bear.

11. Sin yields its pleasure first; but the pain is *sure* to follow. The pleasures of *sin* are but for a season.

12.  As every grain of gold is precious, so is every moment of time.

13.  As they who, for every slight infirmity, take medicine to repair their health, do rather impair it; so they who, for every trifle, are eager to vindicate their character, do rather weaken it.

14.  Time is more valuable to *young* people than to any *others*. They should not lose an *hour* in forming their *taste*, their *manners*, and their *minds*; for whatever they *are*, to a certain degree, at *eighteen*, they *will be*, in a greater or less degree, *all the rest of their lives*.

15.  View the groves in *autumn* and observe the constant succession of falling *leaves*; in like manner the generations of *men* silently drop from the stage of *life* and are blended with the *dust* from whence they *sprang*.

16.  He who would pass the *latter part* of his life with *honor* and *decency* must, when he is *young*, consider that he shall one day be *old*; and remember, when he is *old*, that he has once been *young*.

17.  *Knowledge* will not be acquired without *pains* and *application*. It is troublesome digging for *deep, pure* waters, but when once you come to the *spring*, they rise up and *meet* you.

18.  There are no principles but those of *religion* to be depended on in cases of *real distress*; and these are able to encounter the worst *emergencies* and to bear us up under all the *changes* and *chances* to which our lives are subject.

QUESTIONS — Reread the Rule of Reading at the beginning of this lesson. Why would it be inappropriate to emphasize the italicized words in the Bible? To answer this question, you must find out why words in the Bible are italicized. You may have to ask a minister or other Bible student. (Use the King James Version for your inquiry. No doubt this was the version used by McGuffey.)

SPELL AND DEFINE — (1) signifies; (2) supernatural; (13) infirmity; (15) generations; (17) acquired, application; (18) emergencies, encounter.

# LESSON XIV (14)

## *The Bible*—S. H. TYNG

RULE—Read for improvement and not for show. The great object of reading is to improve your mind in useful knowledge, to establish your heart in virtue, and to prepare you for a right performance of the duties of life.

The word BIBLE means *book*, and the sacred volume is so called because it is the book of books—the best book. The word SCRIPTURES signifies *writings*. The Bible was not written at one time or by one person; but consists of various parts written at different times by different men. It is divided into two Testaments, called the *Old* and the *New*, chiefly with reference to the time when they were published; the *Old* having been published before the coming of Christ, and the *New* after His death.

The *excellency of the Bible* might be proved sufficiently from its sanctifying and transforming influence upon the minds of all who read it with a proper spirit. But this is manifest more especially from the fact of its having God for its author. That God is its author is evident from its being the only book which teaches everything that our Creator requires of us, either to know, or believe, or do, that we may escape His deserved displeasure, obtain His sovereign favor, and dwell forever in the bliss of His immediate presence.

It opens to us the mystery of the creation; the nature of God, of angels and of men; the end for which man was created; the origin of evil; the inseparable connection between sin and misery; the vanity of the present world; and the glory reserved in a future state for the pious servants of God.

Although many hundreds of thousands of books have been written in different ages by wise and learned men, even the best of them will bear no comparison with the Bible in respect either to religion, morality, history or purity and sublimity of composition. Perhaps no man was ever better qualified to pronounce his judgment in this matter than the late Sir William Jones* who was one of the most learned men that ever lived.

He says, "I have regularly and attentively read the Holy Scriptures and am of the opinion that this volume, independent of its divine origin, contains more true sublimity, more exquisite beauty, purer morality, more important history, and finer strains, both of poetry and eloquence, than could be collected within the same compass, from all other books that were ever composed in any age or nation. The antiquity of these compositions no man doubts; and the unstrained application of them to events long subsequent to their publication is a solid ground of belief that they were genuine predictions, and consequently inspired."

The *antiquity of the Bible* is universally acknowledged. The evidences of its having existed from very remote ages are more numerous and convincing than can be adduced in favor of any other book in existence. It has never been without its intelligent witnesses and zealous guardians, though some of them have been the greatest perverters of its peculiar principles or the bitterest enemies of the Christian name.

The Old Testament has been preserved by the Jews in every age, with a scrupulous jealousy and with a veneration for its words and letters, bordering on superstition and demonstrating their regard for it as divinely inspired. The Hebrews never were guilty of negligence in relation even to the *words* of their sacred books, for they used to transcribe and compare them so carefully that they could tell how many times every letter was used in writing any book of the Old Testament.

The books of Moses, including Genesis, Exodus, Leviticus, Numbers and Deuteronomy, were written more than three thousand, three hundred years ago, and nearly fifteen hundred years before the Christian era. Many of the other books were published above a thousand years, and those of the elder prophets about eight hundred years before the advent of Christ.

The writings of all uninspired men are modern compared with the Holy Scriptures.** The earliest history, which is known, is that of Herodotus, written in Greek and written no earlier than the time of Malachi, the last of the Old Testament writers. Somewhat more ancient than Herodotus, are the poems of Homer and Hesiod. The period in which they were written cannot be correctly ascertained, but those who allow them the remotest antiquity, place Homer only in the days of Isaiah the prophet and Hesiod in the age of Elijah.

The books of these ancient, uninspired writers are of quite a different character from the Holy Scriptures. They are filled with silly and absurd fables and contain many impurities. They make no discovery of the just character of the only living and true God, though they contain much concerning religion. As to the history of Herodotus, it contains much that is merely fabulous and untrue, but as far as it records the transactions of his own age, or describes the things within the compass of his own observation, or details matter of fact, of which he was correctly informed, his statements confirm the faithfulness and accuracy of the records contained in the holy and inspired word of the Lord.

The *inspiration of the Holy Scriptures* is evident from their divine sentiments in religion, the glorious character under which they represent Almighty God, the purity and reasonableness of their morality, the majestic simplicity of their style, their wonderful efficacy on the minds of believers, the faithfulness and disinterestedness of the writers, the miracles by which they confirmed their doctrines, the astonishing preservation of the several books to our times, and the fulfillment of their numerous and various prophecies.

The books of the Old Testament, in the number and order in which we now possess them, were held sacred by the Jewish church. Concerning them especially the apostle Paul declares, "All Scripture is given by inspiration of God," and the apostle Peter in reference to the same, testifies, "No prophecy of the Scripture is of any private interpretation. For the prophecy came not in old time by the will of man: but holy men of God spake as they were moved by the Holy Ghost."

To be inspired of God means to be supernaturally influenced by His Holy Spirit. Thus the ancient prophets are said to have spoken by divine inspiration. The inspiration of the sacred writers consisted, 1. In their being infallibly excited and moved to undertake their work; 2. In being furnished by special revelation from God with the knowledge of things which they had not previously possessed;

3. In being directed in the choice of proper words to express their conceptions; and, 4. In being guided in all things to write according to the will of God.

The sovereign goodness of God has been singularly manifested in the wisdom and skill with which He has endowed His servants in relation to His inspired word. Through His gracious providence, the Holy Scriptures have not only been preserved down to our time, but they have been translated into our language by pious and devoted men. And by the same providence, skillful mechanics have been led to discover the wonderful art of printing, by which means the Bible has now become the most common book among us, while four hundred years ago a copy cost a large sum of money, and not without difficulty could it be obtained at all.

• • •

*Chief Justice of the Supreme Court in Calcutta, born 1748; died, much lamented, 1794.

**Since the publication of the McGuffey Readers, archaeologists have unearthed writings that are older than those of the Bible. The most notable discovery, made in 1975, has been the clay tablets of Ebla. Written sometime between 2700 and 2200 B.C., these tablets relate Ebla's economic and political development and also include information about its laws and religion. Although these writings predate the earliest Old Testament writings, this fact does not affect the basic logic of this lesson because Ebla's clay tablets were unknown from the time of their burial until 1975, and therefore, they had no influence on the development of civilization.

QUESTIONS — 1. What is the meaning of the word *Bible*? 2. How may the excellency of the Bible be proved? 3. How do the ancient uninspired writings differ from the Holy Scriptures?

SPELL AND DEFINE — (2) transforming, excellency; (5) morality; (6) adduced, antiquity; (7) superstition; (9) uninspired; (10) fabulous; (12) inspiration; (13) supernaturally.

# LESSON XV (15)

## *More About the Bible*

RULE—As we cannot read well what we do not understand, we need to study what seems difficult and look in a dictionary for the pronunciation of all hard words. But it is the context that can give the *true meaning* of words as they are found in a sentence.

The *design of the Bible* is evidently to give us correct information concerning the creation of all things by the omnipotent word of God, to make known to us the state of holiness and happiness of our first parents in paradise and their dreadful fall from that condition by transgression against God, which is the original cause of all our sin and misery.

It is also designed to show us the duty we owe to Him who is our almighty Creator, our bountiful Benefactor, and our righteous Judge; and the method by which we can secure His eternal friendship and be prepared for the possession of everlasting mansions in His glorious kingdom.

The Scriptures are especially designed to make us wise unto salvation through faith in Christ Jesus; to reveal to us the mercy of the Lord in Him; to form our minds after the likeness of God our Savior; to build up our souls in wisdom and faith, in love and holiness; to make us thoroughly furnished unto good works, enabling us to glorify God on earth; and finally to be glorified with Christ in heaven.

If such be the design of the Bible, how necessary must it be for everyone to pay a serious and proper attention to what it reveals. The word of God invites our attentive and prayerful regards in terms the most engaging and persuasive. It closes its gracious appeals by proclaiming, "Whosoever will, let him take the water of life freely." The infinite tenderness of the divine compassion to sinners flows in the language of the inspired writers, and the most gracious promises of the Lord of glory accompany the divine invitation.

We have the most ample and satisfactory proofs that the books of the Bible are *authentic* and *genuine*: that is, that they were written by the persons to whom they are ascribed. The scriptures of the Old Testament were collected and completed under the scrupulous care of inspired apostles. The singular providence of God is evident in the translation of the Old Testament into Greek nearly three hundred years before the birth of Christ, for the benefit of the Jews who were living in countries where that language was used.

The testimony which our Savior bore to the Old Testament used by the Jews in Judea and the quotations which the New Testament writers have made from its several books, generally from the Greek translation, confirm what has been already said on the antiquity of the Bible and prove its authenticity.

This will appear in a much stronger point of view when we consider the Jews as the keepers of the Old Testament. It was their own sacred volume which contained the most extraordinary predictions concerning the infidelity of their nation and the rise, progress and extensive prevalence of Christianity.

That all the books which convey to us the history of the events of the New Testament were written and immediately published by persons living at the time of the occurrence of the things mentioned, and whose names they bear, is most fully proved — 1. By an unbroken series of Christian authors, reaching from the days of the apostles down to the present time. 2. By the concurrent and well-informed belief of all denominations of Christians. 3. By the acknowledgment of the most learned and intelligent enemies of Christianity.

That the books we possess under the titles of Matthew, Mark, Luke, and John were written by the persons whose names they bear, cannot be doubted by any well-informed and candid mind because from the time of their first publication, they have been uniformly attributed to them by all Christian writers. That all the facts related in these writings and all the accounts given of our Savior's actions and sayings are strictly true, we have the most substantial grounds for believing.

Matthew and John were two of our Lord's apostles, His constant attendants throughout the whole of His ministry, eye-witnesses of the facts and ear-witnesses of the discourses which they relate. Mark and Luke were not of the twelve apostles, but they were contemporaries and associates with the apostles and living in habits of friendship and communication with those who had been present at the events which they record.

As to the preservation of the sacred books down to our times, it is certain, that although the original copies may have been lost, the books of the New Testament have been preserved without any material alteration, much less corruption, and that they are, in all essential matters, the same as when they came from the hands of their authors. In taking copies of these books by writing, from time to time, as the art of printing was then unknown, some letters, syllables, or even words, may have been omitted, altered, or even changed in some manuscripts; but no important doctrine, precept or passage of history has been designedly or fraudulently corrupted.

This would have been impossible because, as soon as the original writings were published, great numbers of copies were immediately taken, carried by the evangelical missionaries wherever they went, and sent to the different churches. They were soon translated into foreign languages and conveyed into the most distant countries. They were constantly read in the Christian assemblies, diligently perused by many private Christians, some of whom had whole books by heart. They were quoted by numerous writers and appealed to as the inspired standard of doctrine by various sects who differed from each other on some important points. Consequently, they were jealously watchful against the least attempt either to falsify or to alter the word of divine revelation.

The manuscripts of the sacred books are found in every ancient library in all parts of the Christian world, and amount to several thousands. About five hundred have been actually examined and compared by learned men with extraordinary care. Many of them were evidently transcribed as early as the eighth, seventh, sixth, and even the fourth centuries.

Thus we are carried up to very near the times of the apostles and the first promulgation of the inspired writings. The prodigious number of these manuscripts, the remote countries whence they have been collected, and the identity of their contents with the quotations which the fathers of different ages have made, demonstrate the authenticity of the New Testament. It has been indeed asserted by learned men that if the New Testament were lost, its contents might be wholly supplied by the quotations from it, which are found in the writings of the fathers of the first four centuries of the Christian church.

QUESTIONS — 1. For what purposes was the Bible designed? 2. What is confirmed by the quotations of Jesus from the Old Testament? 3. Why would alterations in the Bible have been detected? 4. How can you tell whether people today value the sacred scriptures?

SPELL AND DEFINE — (1) omnipotent; (2) everlasting; (3) salvation; (5) translation; (6) quotation; (7) predictions; (8) acknowledgment; (10) contemporaries; (11) manuscripts; (12) evangelical; (14) promulgation, authenticity.

# LESSON XVI (16)

## *Musical Mice*

RULE—In reading long sentences you must not wait for the end to take a breath. You may breathe at a comma or semicolon very conveniently.

On a rainy evening as I was alone in my room, I took up my flute and began to play a tune. In a few minutes my attention was directed to a mouse that I saw creeping from its hole and advancing to the chair in which I was sitting.

I ceased playing, and it suddenly ran back to the hole. I began again shortly afterward and was much surprised to see it return and take its old position. The appearance of the little animal was truly delightful. It crouched itself on the floor, shut its eyes, and appeared in an ecstasy.

I ceased playing, and it instantly disappeared again. This experiment I repeated frequently with the same success, observing that it was always differently affected as the music varied from the slow and plaintive to the brisk and lively. It finally went off, and all my arts to entice it to return were unavailing. Such frequent and powerful excitements probably caused its death.

A more remarkable instance of this fact appeared in one of the public journals not long ago. It was communicated by a gentleman who was a witness of this interesting scene: As a few officers on board a British man-of-war in the harbor of Plymouth were seated around the fire, one of them began to play a very plaintive air on the violin.

He had performed but a few minutes, when a mouse, apparently frantic, made its appearance in the middle of the floor. The strange gestures of the little animal strongly excited the attention of the company, who with one consent, resolved to suffer it to continue its singular actions unmolested.

Its exertions now appeared to be greater every moment. It shook its head, leaped about the floor, and exhibited signs of the most ecstatic delight. It was observed that in proportion as the tones of the instrument approached the soft and plaintive, the feelings of the animal appeared to be increased.

After performing actions which an animal so diminutive would seem at first sight to be incapable of performing, the little creature, to the astonishment of the hitherto delighted spectators, suddenly ceased to move, fell down and expired without showing any signs of pain.

QUESTIONS — 1. In the two incidents related here, what two musical instruments were played? 2. How did the mice, in each case, react to the music—as it began or stopped and as its tempo changed? 3. Evidently, what was the ultimate effect of the music on the mice?

SPELL AND DEFINE — (2) position, crouched; (3) plaintive, excitements; (4) man-of-war; (5) unmolested; (6) ecstatic; (7) diminutive.

# LESSON XVII (17)

## *Character of Jesus Christ*
### BISHOP PORTEUS

RULE—In most words the letter *h* is pronounced, but in a few words, such as *heir* and *herb*, it is not. Learn when to pronounce the *h* and when not to.

The morality taught by Jesus Christ was purer, sounder, sublimer, and more perfect than had ever before entered into the imagination or proceeded from the lips of man. And this He delivered in a manner most striking and impressive—in short, sententious, solemn, important, ponderous rules or maxims or in familiar, natural comparisons and parables.

He showed also a most consummate knowledge of the human heart and dragged to light all its artifices, subtleties, and evasions. He discovered every thought as it arose in the mind. He detected every irregular desire before it ripened into action.

He manifested, at the same time, the most perfect impartiality. He had no respect of persons. He reproved vice in every social class with the same freedom and boldness wherever He found it; and He added to the whole, the weight—the irresistible weight—of His own example.

He, and He only, of all the sons of men, lived up to, in every minute instance, what He taught. His life exhibited a perfect portrait of His religion. But what completed the whole was, that He taught as the evangelist expresses it, *with authority*, with the authority of a divine teacher.

The ancient philosophers could do nothing more than give good advice to their followers; they had no means of enforcing that advice, but our great lawgiver's precepts are all *divine commands*.

He spoke in the name of God. He called Himself the Son of God. He spoke in a tone of superiority and authority, which no one before Him had the courage or the right to assume. And finally, He enforced everything He taught by the most solemn and awful sanctions—by a promise of eternal felicity to those who obeyed Him and a denunciation of the most tremendous punishments to those who rejected Him.

These were the circumstances which gave our blessed Lord the authority with which He spoke. No wonder then, that the people "were astonished at his doctrines," and that they all declared "he spake as never man spake."

QUESTIONS — 1. How do the teachings of Jesus differ from the teachings of all ancient and modern philosophers? 2. Why did Jesus speak and teach with such authority? 3. The morality that Jesus taught was concerned not only with behavior but also motive. Find in your Bible two examples of Jesus' concern for motive. (He often expressed the idea of motive with the word *heart*.)

SPELL AND DEFINE — (1) morality, sententious; (2) consummate; (3) irresistible; (6) denunciation; (7) doctrines.

# LESSON XVIII (18)

## *Clothing of Animals and Vegetables*

RULE—Readers are sometimes in the habit of separating the final consonant of a word from the word to which it belongs, and affixing it to the word succeeding when that succeeding word begins with a vowel. For example, saying *mos tov* for *most of*, or *habi tov* for *habit of*.

Most of the animals, by an admirable contrivance of the Creator, are covered with wool, fur, hair, or feathers. All these are among the number of substances which are bad conductors of heat, and thus keep it from escaping. They are clothed by the hand of Providence exactly in conformity with their wants and the nature of things.

Their dress accommodates itself to the heat of summer and the cold of winter. It falls and becomes thin in the former period and grows thicker during the winter. The aquatic birds have a species of very warm down, which only covers that part of their breast exposed to the water, and their feathers are varnished with a bland oil. This protection at once fortifies them against cold and humidity.

Nature carries her foresight still further. The same animal acquires a different fur in different climates. The northern frosts impart to the goat, rabbit, cat, and sheep a thick and furry vestment. The same animals are almost deprived of hair in the burning regions of Senegal Guinea; while in Syria, according to the expression of a naturalist, they are covered with a long, light and silky vestment like the robe of the Orientals.

The wants of all beings have been calculated with such an exactness of benevolent justice, that the animals which live in valleys where they enjoy a milder temperature are more thinly clad than the mountain animals that wander in the midst of storms and snow.

We might trace the same wise arrangement even in the conformation of vegetables. Their flower buds are destined to multiply and perpetuate the species. They contain at the same time the seed, the fruit, and the coming tree. Nature, neglecting nothing that could tend to preserve so important a charge, has fenced the bud with scales, overlaying one another like tiles; bristled them with hairs which defend them from insects; and lubricated them with a light varnish, over which the water glides without leaving a trace of humidity.

As animals are more warmly clad by nature, in proportion as their climates are colder, so, as we approach the warmer countries, these scales which envelop the germs diminish by degrees and end by disappearing entirely.

In the torrid zone the light buds of flowers are naked, like the native that dances around the tree which bears them. Transfer this vegetable to our climates, and you will see nature take care to clothe and defend it by numerous scales. This is her process of acclimation.

Everything in the universe perishes, but only to be renewed. Nature incessantly struggles against destruction, and her wise and benevolent foresight maintains the equilibrium between life and death. What admirable precaution has she taken to secure the reproduction of the humblest plant!

During the close of summer, she covers the ears of our corn with husks, more or less thick, according to the mildness or severity of the winter that is to follow. The naturalist discovers this provident care in many of the coverings of the fruits and grains.

The native counts the number and thickness of these coats and is forewarned for what severity of winter he has to prepare. Although unread in the lore of our books, by reading the beautiful book of nature, he is enabled to regulate his labors, his hunting and fishing in the desert.

I hope you have seen that the study of nature is full of charms. In proportion as you investigate her secrets, the wisdom of Providence is continually disclosed, and your views become more broad and delightful, and all dryness disappears from the pursuit of knowledge. You enjoy such a pleasure as the traveler experiences, who has finally toiled to the summit of a mountain. The boundless prospect opens before him, and the heavens surround him on all sides.

QUESTIONS — 1. How do animals of the same species differ in northern and southern climates? 2. What are some of the various ways that nature provides for the reproduction of plants? 3. What are some benefits you could receive from studying the things of nature?

SPELL AND DEFINE — (1) conductors; (2) bland, aquatic, humidity; (3) naturalist; (5) conformation; (7) torrid zone; (8) equilibrium, benevolent; (11) boundless.

# LESSON XIX (19)

## *The Lost Child*—ABBOTT

RULE—In order to make your reading appear as much as possible like good speaking or conversation, it is necessary to look at the persons to whom you read, when you can do it without making mistakes.

A few years ago a child was lost in the woods. He was out with his brothers and sisters gathering berries and was accidentally separated from them and lost. The children, after looking in vain for some time in search of the little wanderer, returned just in the dusk of the evening to inform their parents that their brother was lost and could not be found.

The woods at that time were infested with bears. The darkness of a cloudy night was rapidly coming on, and the alarmed father, gathering a few of his neighbors, hastened in search of the lost child. The mother remained at home, almost distracted with suspense.

As the clouds gathered and the darkness increased, the father and the neighbors, with highly-excited fears, traversed the woods in all directions and raised loud shouts to attract the attention of the child. But their search was in vain. They could find no trace of the wanderer; and as they stood under the boughs of the lofty trees and listened, that if possible, they might hear his feeble voice, no sound was borne to their ears but the melancholy moaning of the wind as it swept through the thick branches of the forest.

The gathering clouds threatened an approaching storm, and the deep darkness of the night had already enveloped them. It is difficult to conceive what were the feelings of that father. And who could imagine how deep the agony which filled the bosom of that mother as she heard the wind and beheld the darkness in which her child was wandering!

The search continued in vain until nine o'clock in the evening. Then one of the party was sent back to the village to collect the inhabitants for a more extensive search. The bell rang the alarm, and the cry of fire resounded through the streets. It was, however, ascertained that it was not fire which caused the alarm, but that the bell tolled the more solemn tidings of a lost child.

Every heart sympathized in the sorrows of the distracted parents. Soon multitudes of the people were seen ascending the hill upon the slope of which the village was situated, to aid in the search. Ere long the rain began to fall, but no tidings came back to the village of the lost child. Hardly an eye was that night closed in sleep, and there was not a mother who did not feel for the agonized parents.

The night passed away and the morning dawned, and yet no tidings came. At last those engaged in the search met together and held a consultation. They made arrangements for a more minute and extended search and agreed that in case the child was found, a gun should be fired to give a signal to the rest of the party.

As the sun arose the clouds were dispelled, and the whole landscape glittered in the rays of the bright morning. But that village was deserted and still. The stores were closed, and business was hushed. Mothers were walking the streets with sympathizing countenances and anxious hearts. There was but one thought there—What has become of the lost child?

All the affections and interest of the community

were flowing in one deep and broad channel towards the little wanderer. About nine in the morning the signal gun was fired, which announced that the child was found, and for a moment how dreadful was the suspense! Was it found a mangled corpse or was it alive and well?

Soon a joyful shout proclaimed the safety of the child. The shout was borne from tongue to tongue until the whole forest rang again with the joyful acclamations of the multitude. A commissioned messenger rapidly bore the tidings to the distracted mother. A procession was immediately formed by those engaged in the search. The child was placed upon a platform, hastily constructed from the boughs of trees and borne in triumph at the head of the procession. When they arrived at the brow of the hill, they rested for a moment and proclaimed their success with three loud and animated cheers.

The procession then moved on until they arrived in front of the dwelling where the parents of the child resided. The mother, who stood at the door with streaming eyes and throbbing heart, could no longer restrain herself or her feelings.

She rushed into the street, clasped her child to her bosom, and wept aloud. Every eye was filled with tears and for a moment all were silent. But suddenly someone gave a signal for a shout. One loud and long and happy note of joy rose from the assembled multitude—and they then dispersed to their business and their homes.

There was more joy over the one child that was found, than over the ninety and nine that went not astray. Likewise there is joy in the presence of the angels of God over one sinner that repenteth. Still this is but a feeble representation of the love of our Father in heaven for us and of the joy with which the angels welcome the returning wanderer. The mother cannot feel for her child that is lost, as God feels for the unhappy wanderers in the paths of sin.

Oh, if a mother can feel so much, what must be the feelings of our Father in heaven! If man can feel so deep a sympathy, what must be the emotions which glow in the bosoms of angels?

QUESTIONS — 1. What dangers create a feeling of suspense in this story? 2. How did the community rally around the parents and help them? 3. Why would such community-wide involvement be very rare today? 4. This story was written to illustrate something—what is it?

SPELL AND DEFINE — (1) wanderer; (2) suspense; (3) traversed; (6) ascending, sympathized; (10) proclaimed; (11) procession; (12) dispersed; (13) representation.

# LESSON XX (20)

## *The Rainbow*—STURM

RULE—Read with reflection. One lesson read with careful reflection will do more to improve the mind and enrich the understanding than skimming over the surface of a whole book.

When the sun darts his rays on the drops of water that fall from a cloud, and when we are so placed that our backs are towards the sun and the cloud is before us, then we see a rainbow.

The drops of rain may be considered as small, transparent globes on which the rays fall and are twice refracted and once reflected. Hence the colors of the rainbow, which are *seven* in number and are arranged in the following order: red, orange, yellow, green, blue, indigo, and violet.

These colors appear the most vivid when the cloud behind the rainbow is dark and the drops of rain fall thick and fast. The drops falling continually produce a new rainbow every moment, and as each spectator has his particular situation, from which he observes this phenomenon, it so happens that no two people, properly speaking, can see the *same* rainbow. This rainbow can last no longer than the drops of rain continue to fall.

If we consider the rainbow merely as a phenomenon of nature, it is one of the finest sights imaginable. It is the most beautiful colored picture which the Creator has placed before our eyes. But, when we recollect that God has made it a sign of His mercy and of the covenant which He has condescended to enter into with man, then we shall find matter in it for the most edifying reflection.

When the rain is general, there can be no rainbow. As often, therefore, as we see this beautiful symbol of peace, we may conclude with certainty that we need fear no deluge; for to effect one, there must be a violent rain from all parts of the heavens at once.

Thus, when the sky is only covered on one side with clouds, and the sun is seen on the other, it is a proof that these gloomy clouds shall be shortly dispersed, and the heavens become serene. Hence it is that a rainbow cannot be seen unless the sun be behind and the rain before us. For the formation of the bow, it is necessary that the sun and the rain should be seen at the same time.

QUESTIONS — 1. How is a rainbow formed? 2. Although the rainbow is beautiful just as a phenomenon of nature, what adds to its beauty and significance?

SPELL AND DEFINE — (2) transparent, refracted; (3) phenomenon; (4) covenant, condescended; (6) serene, formation.

# LESSON XXI (21)

## *The Rainbow*—CAMPBELL

RULE—Do not allow the measure of poetry, its rhyme and melody, to betray you into a mode of chanting.

The evening was glorious,
    and light through the trees
Play'd the sunshine and raindrops,
    the birds and the breeze.
The landscape, outstretching in loveliness, lay
On the lap of the year, in the beauty of May.

For the Queen of Spring,
    as she passed down the vale,
Left her robe on the trees,
    and her breath on the gale;
And the smiles of her promise
    gave joy to the hours,
And flush, in her footsteps,
    spring herbage and flowers.

The skies, like a banner, in sunset unroll'd,
O'er the west threw their splendor
    of azure and gold;
But one cloud at a distance,
    rose dense, and increas'd
Till its margin of black
    touch'd the zenith and east.

We gaz'd on the scenes,
    while around us they glow'd,
When a vision of beauty appear'd on the cloud,—
'Twas not like the Sun, as at mid-day we view,

Nor the Moon that rolls nightly
    through starlight and blue.


Like a spirit, it came in the van of the storm!
And the eye and the heart
    hailed its beautiful form:
For it look'd not severe like an Angel of Wrath,
But its garment of brightness
    illum'd its dark path.


In the hues of its grandeur, sublimely it stood,
O'er the river, the village, the field, and the wood;
And, river, field, village
    and woodlands grew bright,
As conscious they gave and afforded delight.


'Twas the bow of Omnipotence, bent in His hand,
Whose grasp at Creation the universe spann'd;
'Twas the presence of God, in symbol sublime;
His vow from the flood to the exit of Time!


O! such was the Rainbow, that beautiful one!
Whose arch was refraction, its keystone the Sun;
A pavilion it seemed, which the Deity graced,
And Justice and Mercy met there, and embraced.


Awhile, and it sweetly bent over the gloom,
Like Lover o'er a death-couch,
    or Hope o'er the tomb;
Then left the dark scene; whence it slowly retired,
As Love had just vanished, or Hope had expired.


I gazed not alone on that source of my song;
To all who beheld it, these verses belong;
Its presence to all was the path of the Lord!
Each full heart expanded—grew warm and adored.

Like a visit—the converse of friends—or a day,
That bow, from my sight, passed forever away;
Like that visit, that converse,
　　　that day—to my heart,
That bow from remembrance can never depart.

'Tis a picture in memory, distinctly defined
With the strong and unperishing colors of mind:
A part of my being, beyond my control,
Beheld on that cloud, but transcribed on my soul.

Not dreadful, as when in the whirlwind he pleads,
When storms are His chariot,
　　　and lightning His steeds,
The black clouds His banner
　　　of vengeance, unfurled,
And thunder His voice to a guilt-stricken world:—

In the breath of His presence,
　　　when thousands expire,
And seas boil with fury, and rocks burn with fire,
And the sword, and the plague-spot,
　　　with death strew the plain,
And vultures and wolves
　　　are the graves of the slain.

QUESTIONS — 1. What is called Queen of Spring? 2. In stanza
7 find three names that the poet gives to the rainbow. 3. Differ-
ing from the rainbow, what are some "dreadful" manifestations
of God's presence?

SPELL AND DEFINE — (1) landscape; (6) grandeur; (7) omnipotence; (8) refraction, keystone; (12) transcribed; (13) vengeance.

# LESSON XXII (22)

## *The Dead Mother*

RULE—This kind of composition is called dialogue and requires more care in reading than any other. The tones should not be too familiar, yet still conversational.

Father: Touch not thy mother, boy.
        Thou canst not wake her.

Child: Why, Father?
        She still wakens at this hour.

Father: Your mother's dead, my child.

Child: And what is dead?
        If she be dead, why, then,
          'tis only sleeping,
        For I am sure she sleeps.
          Come, Mother, rise—
        Her hand is very cold!

Father: Her *heart* is cold.
        Her limbs are bloodless;
          would that mine were so!

Child: If she would waken,
          she would soon be warm.
        Why is she wrapt in this thin sheet? If I,
        This winter morning,
          were not covered better,
        I should be cold like her.

Father: No—not like her:
        The fire might warm *you*,
          or thick clothes—
          but *her*—
        Nothing can warm again!

Child: If I could wake her,

She would smile on me
 as she always does,
And kiss me.
 Mother! you have slept too long—
Her face is pale—
 and it would frighten me,
But that I know she loves me.

Father: Come, my child.

Child: Once when I sat upon her lap, I felt
A beating at her side, and then she said
It was her heart that beat,
 and bade me feel
For my own heart,
 and they both beat alike,
Only mine was the quickest—and I feel
My own heart yet—but hers—
 I cannot feel—

Father: Child! child! You drive me mad.
 Come hence, I say.

Child: Nay, Father, be not angry! Let me stay
Here till my mother wakens.

Father: I have told you,
Your mother cannot wake—
 not in this world—
But in another she *will* wake for us.
When we have slept like her,
 then we shall see her.

Child: Would it were night, then!

Father: No, unhappy child!
Full many a night shall pass,
 ere thou canst sleep
That last, long sleep.
 Thy father soon shall sleep it;
Then wilt thou be deserted upon earth;
None will regard thee;
 thou wilt soon forget

That thou hadst natural ties—
    an orphan lone,
Abandoned to the wiles of wicked men.

Child: Father! Father!
Why do you look so terribly upon me,
You will not hurt me?

Father: Hurt thee, darling? No!
Has sorrow's violence so much of anger,
That it should fright my boy?
    Come dearest, come.

Child: You are not angry, then?

Father: Too well I love you.

Child: All you have said,
    I cannot now remember,
Nor what is meant—you terrified me so.
But this I know, you told me—
    I must sleep
Before my mother wakens—
    so, tomorrow—
Oh, Father! that tomorrow
    were but come!

QUESTIONS — This lesson is particularly sad because it points out so vividly the contrasts between the living and the dead, and it shows the young child's lack of understanding about death. 1. What differences between a living person and a dead person are mentioned? 2. What comments does the child make that show he does not understand death?

SPELL AND DEFINE — (10) beating; (15) orphan, abandoned; (16) terribly; (17) violence.

# LESSON XXIII (23)

## *Sermon on the Mount*—BIBLE

RULE—While you are reading the sacred scriptures, you should consider that they are the Word of the Lord and ought therefore, to be read with great attention and seriousness and also more slowly than other writings.

When a word ends with *s*, and the next word begins with *s*, or has much of the sound of *s*, the first words must be pronounced very distinctly before you begin the second. Examples: Theirs is; righteousness' sake; Jesus said; was said.

1.  And seeing the multitude, He went up into a mountain, and when He was sat, His disciples came unto Him.

2.  And He opened His mouth, and taught them, saying,

3.  Blessed are the poor in spirit for theirs is the kingdom of heaven.

4.  Blessed are they that mourn for they shall be comforted.

5.  Blessed are the meek for they shall inherit the earth.

6.  Blessed are they which do hunger and thirst after righteousness for they shall be filled.

7.  Blessed are the merciful for they shall obtain mercy.

8.  Blessed are the pure in heart for they shall see God.

9.  Blessed are the peacemakers for they shall be called the children of God.

10.  Blessed are they which are persecuted for righteousness' sake for theirs is the kingdom of heaven.

11. Blessed are ye when men shall revile you, and persecute you, and shall say all manner of evil against you falsely, for my sake.

12. Rejoice and be exceeding glad; for great is your reward in heaven; for so persecuted they the prophets which were before you.

13. Ye are the salt of the earth, but if the salt have lost its savor, wherewith shall it be salted? It is thenceforth good for nothing, but to be cast out and to be trodden under foot of men.

14. Ye are the light of the world. A city that is set on a hill cannot be hid.

15. Neither do men light a candle, and put it under a bushel, but on a candlestick and it giveth light unto all that are in the house.

16. Let your light so shine before men, that they may see your good works and glorify your Father which is in heaven.

17. Think not that I am come to destroy the law, or the prophets. I am not come to destroy, but to fulfill.

18. For verily I say unto you, till heaven and earth shall pass, one jot or one tittle shall in no wise pass from the law, till all be fulfilled.

19. Whosoever, therefore, shall break one of these least commandments, and shall teach men so, he shall be called the least in the kingdom of heaven; but whosoever shall do, and teach them, the same shall be called great in the kingdom of heaven.

20. For I say unto you, that except your righteousness shall exceed the righteousness of the Scribes and Pharisees, ye shall in no case enter into the kingdom of heaven.

21. Ye have heard that it was said by them of old time, Thou shalt not kill; and whosoever shall kill, shall be in danger of the judgment;

22. But I say unto you, that whosoever is angry with his brother without a cause, shall be in danger of the judgment, and whosoever shall say to his brother, Raca, shall be in danger of the council; but whosoever shall say, thou fool, shall be in danger of hellfire.

23. Therefore, if thou bring thy gift to the altar, and there rememberest that thy brother hath aught against thee,

24. Leave there thy gift before the altar, and go thy way; first be reconciled to thy brother, and then come and offer thy gift.

25. Agree with thine adversary quickly, whilst thou art in the way with him; lest at any time the adversary deliver thee to the judge, and the judge deliver thee to the officer, and thou be cast into prison.

26. Verily I say unto thee, thou shalt by no means come out thence, till thou hast paid the uttermost farthing.

27. Ye have heard that it was said by them of old time, thou shall not commit adultery:

28. But I say unto you that whosoever looketh on a woman to lust after her, hath committed adultery with her already in his heart.

29. And if thy right eye offend thee, pluck it out, and cast it from thee, for it is profitable for thee that one of thy members should perish, and not that thy whole body should be cast into hell.

30. And if thy right hand offend thee, cut it off, and cast it from thee; for it is profitable for thee that one of thy members should perish, and not that thy whole body should be cast into hell.

31. It hath been said, whosoever shall put away his wife, let him give her a writing of divorcement:

32. But I say unto you that whosoever shall put away his wife, saving for the cause of fornication, causeth her to commit adultery, and whosoever shall marry her that is divorced, committeth adultery.

33. Again, ye have heard that it hath been said by them of old time, thou shalt not forswear thyself, but shalt perform unto the Lord thine oaths:

34. But I say unto you, swear not at all, neither by heaven, for it is God's throne:

35. Nor by the earth, for it is His footstool, neither by Jerusalem, for it is the city of the great King:

36. Neither shalt thou swear by the head, because thou canst not make one hair white or black.

37. But let your communication be Yea, yea; Nay, nay; for whatsoever is more than these cometh of evil.

38. Ye have heard that it hath been said, an eye for an eye, a tooth for a tooth.

39. But I say unto you, That ye resist not evil, but whosoever shall smite thee on thy right cheek, turn to him the other also.

40. And if any man will sue thee at the law, and take away thy coat, let him have thy cloak also.

41. And whosoever shall compel thee to go a mile, go with him twain.

42. Give to him that asketh thee, and from him that would borrow of thee, turn not thou away.

43. Ye have heard that it hath been said, thou shalt love thy neighbor and hate thine enemy:

44. But I say unto you, love your enemies, bless them that curse you, do good to them that hate you, and pray for them which despitefully use you and persecute you,

45. That ye may be the children of your Father which is in heaven, for He maketh His sun to rise on the evil and on the good and sendeth rain on the just and on the unjust.

46. For if you love them which love you, what reward have ye? Do not even the publicans the same?

47. And if ye salute your brethren only, what do ye more than others? Do not even the publicans so?

48. Be ye therefore perfect, even as your Father which is in heaven is perfect.

QUESTIONS — 1. In this sermon is Jesus lessening or emphasizing the importance of the law? Give a specific example. 2. Read verses 43–46. a. How should you treat your enemies? b. Why should you treat them this way?

SPELL AND DEFINE — (1) multitude; (3) blessed; (7) merciful; (10) persecuted; (20) Pharisees; (24) reconciled; (25) adversary; (33) forswear; (47) publicans.

# LESSON XXIV (24)

## *Freaks of the Frost*—MISS GOULD

RULE—Let this lesson be read in a brisk and lively manner, being careful, however, not to run one word into another.

The Frost looked forth one still, clear night,
And whispered, "Now I shall be out of sight;
So through the valley and over the height,
　　In silence I'll take my way.
I will not go on like that blustering train,
The wind and the snow, the hail and the rain,
Who make so much bustle and noise in vain,
　　But I'll be as busy as they."

Then he flew to the mountain,
   and powdered its crest,
He lit on the trees, and their boughs he dress'd
In diamond beads—and over the breast
  Of the quivering lake, he spread
A coat of mail, that need not fear
The downward point of many a spear
That he hung on its margin, far and near,
   Where a rock could rear its head.

He went to the window of those who slept,
And over each pane, like a fairy crept;
Wherever he breathed, wherever he stepp'd,
  By the light of the morn were seen
Most beautiful things,
    there were flowers and trees,
There were bevies of birds, and swarms of bees;
There were cities with temples
   and towers, and these
  All pictured in silver sheen!

But he did one thing, that was hardly fair;
He peep'd in the cupboard, and finding there
That all had forgotten for him to prepare,
  "Now just to set them a thinking.
I'll bite this basket of fruit," said he,
"This costly pitcher I'll burst in three;
And the glass of water they've left for me
  Shall 'tchick!' to tell them I'm drinking!"

QUESTIONS — This poem has an interesting rhyme scheme.
Mark it so you can see the pattern. This is how to mark it: Pronounce the last word of the first line (night). Label its sound, A.
Pronounce the last word of the second line (sight). If it rhymes
with the first word, label it with the same letter, if not, label
it B. Continue marking each last word in the stanza. (Use as
many letters of the alphabet as you need.) When you begin a
new stanza, start over with the letter A.

# LESSON XXV (25)

## Stories About the Bear

RULE—Whenever you meet with a parenthesis in reading, read it in a softer and lower tone than you do the other parts of the sentence.

The American black bear lives a solitary life in forests and uncultivated places and subsists on fruits and on the young shoots and roots of vegetables. He is exceedingly fond of honey and, as he is a most expert climber, he scales the loftiest trees in search of it. He delights in fish and is often found in quest of them on the borders of lakes and on the sea-shore. When those resources fail, he will attack small quadrupeds and even animals of some magnitude. Indeed, as is usual in such cases, the love of flesh in him grows with the use of it.

The pursuit of these animals is a matter of the first importance to some of the Indian tribes and is never undertaken without much ceremony. A principal warrior gives a general invitation to all the hunters. This is followed by a strict fast of eight days, in which they abstain from food, but during which the day is passed in continual song.

When they arrive at the hunting ground, they surround as large a space as they can and then contract their circle, searching at the same time every hollow tree and every place capable of being the retreat of a bear. They continue the same practice until the chase is expired.

As soon as a bear is killed, a hunter puts into its mouth a lighted pipe of tobacco, and blowing into it, fills the throat with the smoke, conjuring the spirit of the animal not to resent what they are about to do to its body or to render their future chase unsuccessful.

As the beast makes no reply, they cut out the string of the tongue and throw it into the fire. If it crackles and shrivels up, (which it is almost sure to do), they accept this as a good omen. If not, they consider that the spirit of the beast is not appeased and that the chase of the next year will be unfortunate.

The grizzly bear, like the American black bear, inhabits the northern part of America, but unlike him, he is, perhaps, the most formidable of all bears in magnitude and ferocity. He averages twice the bulk of the black bear, to which, however, he has some resemblance. His teeth are of great size and power. His feet are enormously large. The talons sometimes measure more than six inches.

The neighborhood of the Rocky Mountains is one of the principal haunts of this animal. There, amidst woods and plains and tangled thickets of boughs and underwood, he reigns as much the monarch as the lion is of the sandy wastes of Africa. Even the bison cannot withstand his attack. Such is his muscular strength, that he will drag this ponderous animal to a convenient spot, where he digs a pit for its reception.

The Indians regard him with the utmost terror. His extreme tenacity of life renders him still more dangerous, for he can endure repeated wounds which would be instantaneously mortal to other beasts, and in that state can rapidly pursue his enemy. So that the hunter who fails to shoot him through the brain is placed in a most perilous situation.

One evening the men in the hindmost of one of Lewis and Clark's canoes perceived one of these bears lying in the open ground about three hundred paces from the river. And six of them, who were all good hunters, went to attack him. Concealing themselves by a small eminence, they were able to approach within forty paces unperceived. Four of the hunters now fired, and each lodged a bullet in his body, two of which passed directly through the lungs.

The bear sprang up and ran furiously with open mouth upon them. Two of the hunters, who had reserved their fire, gave him two additional wounds, and one breaking his shoulder blade, somewhat retarded his motions. Before they could again load their guns, he came so close on them, that they were obliged to run towards the river, and before they had gained it, the bear had almost overtaken them.

Two men jumped into the canoe. The other four separated, and concealing themselves among the willows, fired as fast as they could load their pieces. Several times the bear was struck, but each shot seemed only to direct his fury towards the hunters. At last he pursued them so closely that they threw aside their guns and pouches and jumped from a perpendicular bank, twenty feet high, into the river.

The bear sprang after them and was very near the hindmost man when one of the hunters on the shore shot him through the head and finally killed him. When they dragged him on shore, they found that eight bullets had passed through his body in different directions.

On another occasion, the same enterprising travelers met with the largest bear of this species they had ever seen. When they fired, he did not attempt to attack, but fled with a tremendous roar, and such was his tenacity of life, that although five balls had passed through the lungs and five other wounds were inflicted, he swam more than half across the river to a sandbar and survived more than twenty minutes.

QUESTIONS — 1. How did the Indians prepare for a bear hunt? 2. What characteristic of the grizzly bear is being illustrated by the stories of the Lewis and Clark expedition hunters? 3. Do you think it is great sport and an evidence of courage for hunters today to kill the grizzly bear? Why or why not?

SPELL AND DEFINE — (1) uncultivated; (6) ferocity; (8) instantaneously, tenacity; (9) perceived, concealing; (11) perpendicular; (13) enterprising.

# LESSON XXVI (26)

## *On Speaking the Truth*—ABBOTT

RULE—Too much pain cannot be taken to acquire familiarity with the punctuation.

A little girl once came into the house and told her mother a story about something which seemed very improbable.

The persons who were sitting in the room with her mother did not believe the little girl, for they did not know her character. But the mother replied at once, "I have no doubt that it is true, for I never knew my daughter to tell a lie." Is there not something noble in having such a character as this?

Must not that little girl have felt happy in the consciousness of thus possessing her mother's entire confidence? Oh, how different must have been her feelings from those of the child whose word cannot be believed, and who is regarded by everyone with suspicion? Shame, shame on the child who has not magnanimity enough to tell the truth.

There are many ways of being guilty of falsehood without uttering the lie directly in words. Whenever you try to deceive your parents in doing that which you know they disapprove, you do in reality tell a lie. Conscience reproves you for falsehood.

Once when I was in company, as the plate of cake was passed around, a little boy who sat by the side of his mother, took a much larger piece than he knew she would allow him. She happened, for the moment, to be looking away, and he broke a small piece off, and covered the rest in his lap with his handkerchief. When his mother looked, she saw the small piece and supposed he had taken no more. He intended to deceive her. His mother has never found out what he did.

But God saw him at the time. And do you not think that the boy has already suffered for it? Must he not feel mean and contemptible, whenever he thinks that, merely to get a little bit of cake, he would deceive his kind mother? If that little boy had one particle of honorable or generous feeling remaining in his bosom, he would feel reproached and unhappy whenever he thought of his meanness. If he was already dead to shame, it would show that he had by previous deceit acquired such a character.

And can anyone love or esteem a child who has become so degraded? And can a child, who is neither beloved nor respected, be happy? No! You may depend upon it, that when you see a person guilty of such deceit, he does, in some way or other, even in this world suffer a severe penalty. A frank and open-hearted child is the only happy child. Deception, however skillfully it may be practiced, is disgraceful and ensures sorrow and contempt.

If you would have the approbation of your own conscience, and the approval of friends, never do that which you shall desire to have concealed.

Always be open as the day. Be above deceit and then you will have nothing to fear. There is something delightful in the magnanimity of a perfectly sincere and honest child. No person can look upon such a one without affection. With this, you are sure of friends, and your prospects of earthly usefulness and happiness are bright.

You know it is written in the Bible, "God will bring every work into judgment, with every secret thing, whether it be good or whether it be evil." How must the child then feel who has been guilty of falsehood and deception, and who sees it then all brought to light! No liar can enter the kingdom of heaven. Oh, how dreadful must be the confusion and shame with which the deceitful child will then be overwhelmed! The angels will all see your sin and your disgrace.

And do you think they will wish to have a liar enter heaven and be associated with them? No! They will turn from you with disgust. The Savior will look upon you in His displeasure. Conscience will rend your soul. And you must hear the awful sentence, "Depart from me, into everlasting fire, prepared for the devil and his angels."

Oh, it is a dreadful thing to practice deceit. It will shut you out from heaven. Though you should escape detection as long as you live, though you should die and your falsehood not be discovered, the time will soon come when it will be brought to light and when the whole universe—men and angels will be witnesses of your shame.

QUESTIONS — 1. What are the rewards for one who always tells the truth? 2. What are the punishments for one who lies?

SPELL AND DEFINE — (2) character; (3) consciousness, confidence; (4) falsehood; (6) contemptible; (7) disgraceful; (8) magnanimity; (10) liar; (11) deceit.

# LESSON XXVII (27)

## *Advantages of Reading*—HAWES

RULE—Be careful always to read in such a way that you may be distinctly heard. This will depend more upon the distinctness with which you articulate the words than upon the force and loudness of your voice.

It is the glory of man that the Creator has made him capable of endless improvement in knowledge, virtue, and happiness. And it is the high privilege of those who dwell in this favored land, that they enjoy in rich abundance the means of such improvement. Among these means, books hold a prominent place.

But as books are of very various character, some good, some indifferent, and some of a positively pernicious tendency, it is plainly a matter of great importance to make a wise selection of them and to read them with due caution. Especially is this true in regard to young persons and those to whom the active duties of life leave but little leisure for reading.

One book read thoroughly and with careful reflection will do more to improve the mind and enrich the understanding, than skimming over the surface of a whole library. Indeed, the more one reads in this hasty, superficial manner, the worse. It is like loading the stomach with a great quantity of food which lies there undigested. It enfeebles the intellect and pours darkness and confusion over all the operations of the mind.

It is a maxim, then, ever to be born in mind, to *"take heed what you read."* To acquire useful information, to improve the mind in knowledge, and the heart in goodness; to become qualified to perform with honor and usefulness the duties of life; to be prepared for a happy life in eternity—these are the great objects which ought to be kept in view in reading.

Taking this as the criterion by which to regulate your choice of books, you will, I think, be led to give an important place to *historical reading*, especially to that which relates to our own country. History is the mirror of the world. In it we behold the origin and progress of society, the rise and fall of empires. We see, as in a moving picture, the generations of our race as they have risen into being, acted their part on the stage of life, and passed in rapid succession beyond that destination from whence no traveller returns.

Such scenes contemplated in the light of authentic history are replete with the most interesting and profitable lessons. Especially are they so when they relate to our own country. With the history of our own country, every American citizen should be familiar. It is the history of a new world, of a new state of society established for new purposes, developing new views of the character and destiny of man, and marked in every stage of its progress with the most signal interpositions of a gracious and all-pervading Providence.

Nearly related to history, and not less important, is *biography*. This is a kind of reading most happily adapted to minds of every capacity and degree of improvement. While it possesses a charm that can hardly fail to interest the feelings and engage the attention even of the most incurious and least instructed, it furnishes lessons of wisdom and prudence by which the wisest and best may be profited.

It makes you acquainted with the fairest and most excellent specimens of human character. It introduces you into the society of the great and the learned, the wise and the good; you mingle and associate with them in all their walks and ways; you hear them converse; you see them act; and you mark the steps by which they attained their excellence and rose to their elevation in honor and influence.

The effect of this cannot be otherwise than eminently happy. While conversant with such characters, a process of assimilation will be going on in your own minds. You will feel within you an influence, raising you above whatever is base and polluting, and inspiring in you the love of whatever is noble and excellent.

Few authors can be read with more profit than those that illustrate the natural sciences and show their application to the practical arts of life. Authors of this character teach us to read and understand the divine volume of creation. They show us the admirable structure of nature and unfold to our view the beauty, order, and harmony which characterize the works of God.

While in the study of these works, our minds are invigorated, our hearts improved, our views enlarged, and the sources of our enjoyment multiplied. We rise to the contemplation of the Great Being who created and governs all and are thus taught to look through nature, up to nature's God. This is the natural tendency, and this the actual effect in every pious mind, of studying the works of creation.

Who can survey the wondrous volume which the Creator has spread out before us—who can contemplate the earth beneath or read the shining lines of glory and of grandeur, which are inscribed on the heavens above, without exclaiming with the devout Psalmist, "O Lord, how manifold are thy works! in wisdom hast thou made them all; the earth is full of thy riches"?

QUESTIONS — 1. Why should you choose carefully the books you read? 2. What are the chief purposes for reading? 3. Why is biography a valuable kind of book to read? 4. What should the reading of natural sciences cause you to contemplate?

SPELL AND DEFINE — (1) prominent; (2) tendency, pernicious; (5) historical; (6) developing; (9) inspiring; (10) illustrate; (11) contemplation; invigorated.

# LESSON XXVIII (28)

## *Solomon's Wise Choice*—BIBLE

RULE—When a sentence in quoted in the Bible, it is distinguished by being begun with a capital letter and not by the usual quotation marks, as in the first paragraph below: God said, Ask what I shall give thee. *Thee* and *thou* are used for *you*, *art* for *are*, *dost* for *do*. This manner of writing is called the *solemn style* and is frequently used in prayer and in some other cases.

### I Kings 3

5. In Gibeon the Lord appeared to Solomon in a dream by night, and God said, Ask what I shall give thee. And Solomon said, Thou has shewed unto thy servant David, my father, great mercy, according as he walked before thee in truth, and in righteousness, and in uprightness of heart with thee; and thou hast kept for him this great kindness, that thou hast given him a son to sit on his throne, as it is this day.

7. And now O Lord, my God, thou has made thy servant king instead of David my father; and I am but a little child. I know not how to go out or to come in. And thy servant is in the midst of thy people, which thou hast chosen, a great people, that cannot be numbered nor counted for multitude.

9. Give therefore thy servant an understanding heart to judge thy people, that I may discern between good and bad; for who is able to judge this thy so great a people? And the speech pleased the Lord, that Solomon had asked this thing.

11. And God said unto him, Because thou hast asked this thing, and hast not asked for thyself long life; neither hast asked riches for thyself, nor hast asked the life of thine enemies; but hast asked for thyself understanding to discern judgment; behold, I have done according to thy words: lo, I have given thee a wise and an understanding heart, so that there was none like thee before thee, neither after thee shall any arise like unto thee.

13. And I have also given thee that which thou hast not asked, both riches and honor; so that there shall not be any among the kings like unto thee all thy days. And if thou wilt walk in my ways, to keep my statutes, and my commandments, as thy father David did walk, then I will lengthen thy days.

15. And Solomon awoke; and, behold, it was a dream.

## I Kings 4:29–31a

And God gave Solomon wisdom and understanding, exceeding much, and largeness of heart, even as the sand that is on the seashore. And Solomon's wisdom excelled the wisdom of all the children of the east country, and all the wisdom of Egypt. For he was wiser than all men.

## I Kings 10

1. And when the queen of Sheba heard of the fame of Solomon concerning the name of the Lord, she came to prove him with hard questions.

2. And she came to Jerusalem with a very great train, with camels that bare spices, and very much gold, and precious stones; and when she was come to Solomon, she communed with him of all that was in her heart. And Solomon told her all her questions: there was not anything hid from the king which he told her not.

4. And when the queen of Sheba had seen all Solomon's wisdom, and the house that he had built, and the meat of his table, and the sitting of his servants, and the attendance of his ministers, and their apparel, and his cup bearers, and his ascent by which he went up into the house of the Lord, there was no more spirit in her.

6. And she said to the king, It was a true report that I heard in mine own land of thy acts and of thy wisdom. Howbeit, I believed not the words, until I came, and mine eyes had seen it; and behold, the half was not told me: thy wisdom and prosperity exceedeth the fame which I heard.

Happy are thy men, happy are these thy servants, which stand continually before thee, and that hear thy wisdom.

QUESTIONS — 1. When God offered to grant Solomon a request, what did he ask for? 2. How did God indicate that He was pleased with Solomon's request? 3. Why did the Queen of Sheba visit King Solomon?

SPELL AND DEFINE — righteousness, discern, statutes, commandments, howbeit, exceedeth.

# LESSON XXIX (29)

## *About the Locust*—HEWLETT

RULE—While you read distinctly, do not give an undue distinction to unimportant words. This is done by small children when they first begin to read and have to pause at each word to make out the next. Older students sometimes read in a similar manner.

The locust appears to have derived its name from a word which signifies to *multiply*, to *become numerous*. The word suggests immense swarms of these insects by which different countries, especially in the East, are infested. There are various species of locusts. Some are more ferocious and destructive than others, though all are destructive and insatiable spoilers.

The general form and appearance of the locust greatly resemble those of the grasshopper, so well known in our country. The common great brown locust is about three inches in length, has two antennae or feelers about an inch long and two pairs of wings. The head and horns are brown; the mouth and insides of the larger legs are bluish.

It has three pairs of legs, the last much longer and stronger than the other two, fortified by thick muscles and well adapted for springing. It has four wings, the anterior springing from the second pair of legs and the posterior from the third.

The back wings are much finer and more expansive than the foremost and are the principal instruments of its flight. The upper side and foremost wings are brown, the former spotted with black, and the latter with dusky spots. The back is defended with a shield of greenish hue. The back wings are of a light brown hue, tinctured with green and nearly transparent.

If the sun is warm and the soil in which the eggs are deposited is dry, there is, perhaps, nothing in creation that multiplies faster than the locust. We are familiar only with the little chirping grasshoppers which we consider harmless and pleasing, but the locusts differ from them not only in size, but in rapidity of flight and the power of injuring mankind by swarming upon the productions of the earth. The quantity of grass which a few grasshoppers can destroy is trifling, but when a swarm of locusts, two or three miles long and several yards deep, settle on a field, the consequences are frightful.

Wherever they settle, they devour all the grain and vegetables and even all the produce of the earth—eating the very bark from the trees and destroying at once the hopes of the husbandman and the labors of the agriculturist. For though their voracity is great, they contaminate a much greater quantity than they consume. Their bite is poisonous to vegetables, and the marks of devastation may be traced for several succeeding seasons.

Happily for us, the coldness of our climate and the humidity of our soil are by no means favorable to their production or inviting to their migratory visits. The annals, however, of every country are marked with the devastations produced by their invading armies, and though they seldom visit Europe in such dangerous swarms as formerly, yet in some of the southern kingdoms they are still formidable.

In the year 1748, they were seen in several parts of England, especially in Norfolk, where they committed serious depredations and spread general consternation. What they are in warmer climates may be gathered from the following communication from a traveler in the East, who witnessed a visitation from these destructive creatures.

"I cannot represent their flight to you better than by comparing it to the flakes of snow in cloudy weather, driven about by the wind. When they alight on the ground to feed, the plains are all covered. They make a murmuring noise when they eat, and in less than two hours they devour all close to the ground; then rising, they let themselves be carried away by the wind. When they fly, though the sun shines ever so brightly, it is no lighter than when most clouded. The air was so full of them that I could not eat in my room without a candle, all the houses being full of them, even the stables, barns, chambers, garrets, and cellars.

"I caused gunpowder and sulphur to be burned to expel them, but all to no purpose. When the door was opened, an infinite number came in, as the others went out, fluttering about. It was a troublesome thing, when a man went abroad, to be hit on the face by these creatures, so that there was no opening of one's mouth, but some would try to get into it."

QUESTIONS — 1. Why does this country not have the great swarms of locusts that are found in some countries of the East? 2. How do the swarms of locusts cause devastation wherever they go?

SPELL AND DEFINE — (1) derived, ferocious; (4) expansive, tinctured; (5) productions; (6) devastation; (7) migratory; (8) depredations; (10) infinite.

# LESSON XXX (30)

## *The Noblest Revenge*
## ENGLISH MAGAZINE

RULE—When you are alone, think of your faults. When you are with others, correct them. This rule will apply to reading and to all things that you do.

"I will be revenged on him—that I will—and make him heartily repent it," said Philip to himself, with a countenance quite red with anger. His mind was so engaged that he did not see Stephen, who happened at that instant to meet him.

"Who is that," asked Stephen, "on whom you intend to be revenged?" Philip, as if awakened from a dream, stopped short, and looking at his friend, soon resumed a smile that was natural to his countenance.

"Ah," said he, "you remember my supplejack, a very pretty cane, which was given me by my father, do you not? Look there. It is in pieces. It was farmer Robinson's son who reduced it to this worthless state."

Stephen very coolly asked him what had induced young Robinson to break it.

"I was walking peaceably along," replied he, "and was playing with my cane by twisting it round my body. By accident, one of the ends slipped out of my hand when I was opposite the gate, just by the wooden bridge where the ill-natured fellow had put down a pitcher of water, which he was taking home from the well.

"It so happened that my cane, in springing back, upset the pitcher, but did not break it. He came up close to me and began to call me names. I assured him that what I had done had happened by accident and that I was sorry for it. Without regarding what I said, he instantly seized my cane and twisted it, as you see. But I will make him repent of it."

"To be sure," said Stephen, "he is a very mean boy and is already very properly punished for being such, since nobody likes him, or will have anything to do with him. He can scarcely find a companion to play with him and is often at a loss for amusement, as he deserves to be. This, properly considered, I think will appear sufficient revenge for you."

"All this is true," replied Philip, "but he has broken my cane. It was a present from my father, and a very pretty cane it was. I offered to fill his pitcher for him again, as I had knocked it down by accident. I will be revenged."

"Now, Philip," said Stephen, "I think you will act better in not paying any attention to him. Be assured he will always be able to do more mischief to you than you choose to do to him. And now I think of it, I will tell you what happened to him not long ago.

"Very unluckily for him, he chanced to see a bee hovering about a flower. He caught it and was going to pull off its wings out of sport, when the insect stung him and flew away in safety to the hive. The pain put him into a furious passion, and like you, he vowed revenge. He accordingly procured a stick and thrust it into the bee hive.

"In an instant, the whole swarm flew out, and alighting upon him, stung him in a hundred different places. He uttered the most piercing cries and rolled upon the ground in the excess of his agony. His father immediately ran to him, but could not put the bees to flight until they had stung him so severely that he was confined several days to his bed.

"Thus, you see, he was not very successful in his pursuit of revenge. I would advise you, therefore, to pass over his insult. He is a mischievous boy and much stronger than you, so that your ability to obtain this revenge may be doubtful."

"I must admit," replied Philip, "that your advice seems very good. So come along with me and I will tell my father the whole matter, and I think he will not be angry with me." They went and Philip told his father what had happened. He thanked Stephen for the good advice he had given his son and gave Philip another cane exactly like the first.

A few days afterward Philip saw this ill-natured boy fall as he was carrying home a heavy log of wood, which he could not lift up again. Philip ran to him and helped him to replace it on his shoulder. Young Robinson was quite ashamed at the thought of this unmerited kindness and heartily repented of his behavior. Philip went home quite satisfied. "This," said he, "is the noblest vengeance I could take, in *returning good for evil*. It is impossible that I should have to repent of it."

QUESTIONS — 1. Both Philip and young Robinson had done something to displease the other. Why was Robinson's act mean-hearted and Philip's was not? 2. How did Philip finally take revenge on Robinson? 3. When someone mistreats you, what is the *noblest revenge* with which you can repay them?

SPELL AND DEFINE — (5) accident; (7) revenge, sufficient, inflict; (9) mischief; (11) immediately; (12) pursuit; (14) unmerited, vengeance, impossible.

# LESSON XXXI (31)

## Character of the Icelanders
### HENDERSON

RULE—It is better to read a little too loudly than in too feeble a tone. Read, therefore, as if you were addressing the most distant person in the room.

The early settlers of Iceland, like those of New England, were a race well fitted to leave a high state of moral feeling and intelligence to their descendants. Many of them were distinguished men of Norway, who preferred exile to oppression at home and who carried to their adopted country the germ of republican institutions and the knowledge that can best uphold them.

The most prominent traits in the Icelanders are a love of their country, hospitality, intelligence, simplicity, and piety. Though social, they are rather disposed to be serious. It would almost seem that happiness and simplicity of character had deserted the sunny skies and fertile fields of southern Europe to nestle among the icy crags and volcanic ruins of the frozen zone.

It is not so much the literary fame of a few select individuals who have enjoyed superior advantages which strikes our attention, as the universal diffusion of the general principles of knowledge among its inhabitants. Though there be only one school in Iceland, and that solitary school is exclusively designed for the education of such as are afterwards to fill offices in church or state, yet it is exceedingly rare to meet with a boy or girl, who has attained the age of nine or ten years, that cannot read and write with ease.

Domestic education is most rigidly attended to. It is no uncommon thing to hear youths, who have never been farther than a few miles from the place where they were born, repeat passages from the Greek and Latin authors. On many occasions, indeed, the common Icelanders discover an acquaintance with the history and literature of other nations which is perfectly astonishing.

A winter evening in an Icelandic family presents a scene in the highest degree interesting and pleasing. Between three and four o'clock the lamp is hung up in the principal apartment, which answers the double purpose of a bedroom and sitting room, and all the members of the family take their places, with their work in their hands, on their respective beds, all of which face each other.

The master or mistress, together with the children or other relatives, occupy the beds at the inner end of the room. The rest are filled by the servants. The work is no sooner begun, than one of the family, selected on purpose, advances to a seat near the lamp and begins the evening lecture, which generally consists of such histories as are to be obtained on the island.

Being but badly supplied with printed books, the Icelanders are under the necessity of copying such as they can get the loan of, which sufficiently accounts for the fact that most of them write a hand equal in beauty to that of the ablest writing masters in other parts of Europe. Some specimens of their Gothic writing are scarcely inferior to copperplate.

The reader is frequently interrupted, either by the head, or some of the more intelligent members of the family, who make remarks on various parts of the story and propose questions with a view to exercise the ingenuity of the children and servants.

At the conclusion of the evening labors, which are

frequently continued till nearly midnight, the family join in singing a psalm or two, after which, a chapter from some book of devotion is read, if the family does not have a Bible. But where this sacred book exists, it is preferred to every other. A prayer is also read by the head of the family, and the exercise concludes with a psalm. Their morning devotions are conducted in a similar manner.

When the Icelander awakes, he does not salute any person that may have slept in the room with him, but hastens to the door and, lifting up his eyes towards heaven, adores Him who made the heavens and the earth, the Author and Preserver of his being and the Source of every blessing. He then returns into the house and salutes everyone he meets, with, "God grant you a good day!"

There being no parish schools, nor indeed any private establishments for the instruction of youth in Iceland, their mental culture depends entirely on the disposition and abilities of the parents. In general, however, neither of these is lacking, for the natives of this Island are endowed with an excellent natural understanding, and their sense of national honor, founded by their familiar acquaintance with the character and deeds of their forefathers, spurs them to emulation, independent of the still more powerful inducement arising from the necessity and importance of religious knowledge.

The children are taught their letters by their mother or some other woman. And when they have made some progress in reading, they are taught writing and arithmetic by the father. Every clergyman is bound to visit the different families in his parish two or three times a year, on which occasions he teaches both young and old. The exercise is attended to, chiefly with a reference to the former, in order to ascertain what degree of knowledge they possess of the fundamental principles of Christianity.

These are all the means of instruction which the great bulk of the Icelandic youth enjoy; nevertheless, the love of knowledge, introduced by the domestic habits of those who are their superiors in point of age and mental acquirements, often prompts them to build of their own accord on the foundation that has thus been laid. I have frequently been astonished at the familiarity with which many of these self-taught peasants have discourses on subjects, which, in other countries, we should expect to hear started by those only who fill the professor's chair or who have otherwise devoted their lives to the study of science.

QUESTIONS — 1. When this lesson was written (about 150 years ago), how did most Icelandic children receive an education? 2. This lesson attempts to describe a whole nation of people as one group. Can you see any opportunity for an inaccurate impression to be made? Why? 3. Read in an encyclopedia about Iceland and its people today. How has their lifestyle changed from what it was 150 years ago?

SPELL AND DEFINE — (1) descendants; (2) volcanic; (3) diffusion; (4) literature; (7) Gothic; (11) emulation; (13) discoursed, acquirements.

# LESSON XXXII (32)

## *Description of Pompey's Pillar*—IRVING

RULE—Many words in this lesson will oblige the pupil to use his dictionary. Let no word be passed over, which is not understood. The dictionary must be used for the pronunciation, as well as for the meaning. The precise meaning of a word must be gathered from its context.

In visiting Alexandria, what most engages the attention of travelers is the pillar of Pompey, as it is commonly called, situated a quarter of a league from the southern gate. It is composed of red granite. This block of marble, 60 feet in circumference, rests on two layers of stone bound together with lead. This construction has not, however, prevented the Arabs from forcing out several of the rocks to search for an imaginary treasure.

The whole column is 114 feet high. It is perfectly well polished and only a little scarred on the eastern side. Nothing can equal the majesty of this monument. Seen from a distance it overtops the town and serves as a signal for vessels. Approaching it nearer, it produces an astonishment mixed with awe. One can never be tired with admiring the beauty of the capital, the length of the shaft, or the extraordinary simplicity of the pedestal.

This last has been somewhat damaged by the instruments of travelers, who are curious to possess a relic of this antiquity. One of the volutes of the column was immaturely brought down about twelve years ago by a prank of some English captains. The story of this prank is thus related by Mr. Irving:

These jolly sons of Neptune had been pushing about the can on board one of the ships in the harbor, until a strange idea entered into the mind of one of them. The eccentricity of the thought occasioned it immediately to be adopted, and its apparent impossibility was but a spur for putting it into execution.

The boat was ordered, and with proper implements for the attempt, these enterprising heroes pushed ashore to drink a bowl of punch on the top of Pompey's Pillar! They arrived at the spot, and many contrivances were proposed to accomplish the desired point. But their labor was vain, and they began to despair of success, when the fellow who thought of the frolic happily suggested the means of performing it.

A man was dispatched to the city for a paper kite. The inhabitants were by this time made aware of what was going forward and flocked in crowds to be witnesses of the purpose and boldness of the English. The governor of Alexandria was told that those seamen were about to pull down Pompey's Pillar.

But whether he gave them credit for their respect to the Roman warrior, or to the Turkish government, he left them to themselves and politely answered that the English were too great patriots to injure the remains of Pompey. He knew little, however, of the disposition of the people who were engaged in this undertaking. Had the Turkish empire risen in opposition, it would not at that moment have deterred them.

The kite was brought and flown so directly over the Pillar, that when it fell on the other side, the string lodged upon the capital. The chief obstacle was now overcome. A two inch rope was tied to one end of the string and drawn over the pillar by the end to which the kite was affixed.

By this rope one of the seamen ascended to the

top, and in less than an hour a kind of shroud was constructed by which the whole company went up and drank their punch amid the shouts of the astonished multitude. To the eye below, the capital of the pillar does not appear capable of holding more than one man upon it, but the seamen found that it could contain no less than eight persons very conveniently.

It is astonishing that no accident befell these madcaps, in a situation so elevated that it would have turned a landsman giddy in his sober senses. The only detriment which the pillar received, was the loss of the volute before mentioned, which came down with a thundering sound and was carried to England by one of the captains as a present to a lady who had commissioned him for a piece of the pillar.

The discovery which they made amply compensated for this mischief, for, without their evidence, the world would not have known at this time that there was originally a statue on this pillar, one foot and ankle of which are still remaining. The statue must have been of a gigantic size to have appeared with a man's proportions at so great a height.

There are circumstances in this story which might give it an air of fiction were it not authenticated beyond all doubt. Besides the testimony of many eye-witnesses, the adventurers themselves have left us a token of the fact by the initials of their names which are very legible in black paint just below the capital.

QUESTIONS — 1. Locate on a map the city where Pompey's Pillar is. 2. Do you approve of the prank played by the English seamen? Why or why not? 3. Does the writer (Irving) approve? Give an example of his comments showing his attitude. 4. How have people's attitudes about historic monuments changed since this story was written?

SPELL AND DEFINE — (1) league, circumference; (2) column, shaft; (3) volute; (4) eccentricity; (5) frolic; (7) patriots; (10) elevated; (12) authenticated, initials, fiction.

# LESSON XXXIII (33)

## *Anecdote of Birds*—HALL

RULE—In reading, avoid a formal manner and let your method be as much like conversation as possible. *Read* as you would *speak* the same words if you had no book before you.

I had once a favorite black hen. "A great beauty," she was called by everyone, and so I thought her. Her feathers were so jetty and her topping so white and full! She knew my voice as well as any dog and used to run cackling and bustling to my hand to receive the crumbs that I never failed to collect from the breakfast table for "Yarico," as she was called.

Yarico, by the time she was a year old, had hatched a respectable family of chickens—little, cowering, timid things at first, but in due time they became fine chubby ones. Old Nora, the farmer's wife said, "If I could only keep Yarico out of the thicket, it would do, but the thicket is full of weasels and, I am sure, of foxes also. I have driven her back twenty times, but she watches till someone goes out of the gate, and then she's off again. It's always the way with young hens—they think they know better than their keepers, and nothing cures them but losing a brood or two of chickens." I have often thought since then, that young people as well as young hens, buy their experience for a similar costly price.

One morning I went with my crumbs to seek out my favorite in the poultry yard. Plenty of hens were there, but no Yarico! The gate was open and, as I concluded, she had sought the forbidden thicket. I proceeded there, accompanied by the yard mastiff, a noble fellow, steady and sagacious as a judge. At the end of a ragged lane, flanked on one side by a hedge and on the other by a wild common, what was called the thicket began. But before I arrived near the spot, I heard a loud and tremendous cackling and met two young, long-legged pullets, running with both wings and feet towards home. Jock pricked up his sharp ears and would have set off at full gallop to the thicket, but I restrained him, hastening onward, however, at the top of my speed, thinking that I had as good a right to see what was the matter as Jock.

Poor Yarico! An impertinent fox-cub had attempted to carry off one of her children, but she had managed to get them behind her in the hedge, and venturing boldly forth, had placed herself in front and positively kept the impudent animal at bay. His desire for plunder had prevented his noticing our approach, and Jock soon made him feel the superiority of an English mastiff over a cub fox.

The most interesting portion of my tale is to come. Yarico not only never afterwards ventured to the thicket, but formed a strong friendship for the dog who had preserved her family. Whenever he appeared in the yard, she would run to meet him, prating and clucking all the time and impeding his progress by walking between his legs, to his no small annoyance. If any other dog entered the yard, she would fly at him most furiously, thinking, perhaps, that he would injure her chickens, but she evidently considered Jock her special protector and treated him accordingly.

It was very droll to see the peculiar look with which he regarded his feathered friend, not exactly knowing what to make of her civilities and doubting how they should be received. When her family was educated and able to do without her care, she was a frequent visitor at Jock's kennel and would, if permitted, roost there at night instead of returning with the rest of the poultry to the hen house. Yarico certainly was a most grateful and interesting bird.

• • •

One could almost believe the parrot had intellect when he keeps up a conversation so spiritedly. And it certainly is singular to observe how accurately a well-trained bird will apply his knowledge. A friend of mine knew one that had been taught many sentences, thus: "Sally, Poll wants her breakfast!" "Sally, Poll wants her tea!" She never mistook the one for the other. Breakfast was invariably demanded in the morning and tea in the afternoon. And she always hailed her master, but no one else, by "How do you do, Mr. A?"

She was a most amusing bird and could whistle dogs, which she had great pleasure in doing. She would drop bread out of her cage as she hung at the street door and whistle a number about her, and then just as they were going to possess themselves of her bounty, utter a shrill scream of "Get out, dogs!" with such vehemence and authority, as dispersed the assembled company without a morsel—to her infinite delight.

• • •

How wonderful is that instinct, by which the bird of passage performs its annual migration! How still more wonderful is it, when the bird, after its voyage of thousands of miles has been performed, and new lands visited, returns to the precise window or eaves where the summer before it first enjoyed existence! Yet such is unquestionably the fact.

Four brothers had watched with indignation the felonious attempts of the sparrow to possess himself of the nest of the house martin, in which lay its young brood of four unfledged birds.

The little fellows considered themselves as champions for the bird who had come over land and sea and chosen its shelter under their mother's roof. They therefore marshalled themselves with peashooters to execute summary vengeance. But their well-meant endeavors brought destruction upon the mud-built domicil they wished to defend. Their artillery loosened the foundations and down it came, precipitating its four little inmates to the ground. The mother of the children, good Samaritan-like, replaced the little outcasts in their nests, and set it in the open window of an unoccupied room.

The parent birds, after the first terror was over, did not appear disconcerted by the change of situation, but hourly fed their young as usual and testified by their unwearied twitter of the pleasure, the satisfaction, and the confidence they felt. There the young birds were duly fledged and from that window began their flight and entered upon life for themselves.

The next spring, with the reappearance of the martins, came four, who familiarly flew into the chamber, visited all the walls and expressed their recognition by the most clamorous twitterings of joy. They were, without exception, the very birds that had been bred there the preceding year.

QUESTIONS — 1. What finally cured Yarico of running away into the thicket? 2. How did Yarico treat the one that had saved her brood? 3. How did the parrot Poll tease the dogs?

SPELL AND DEFINE — (2) cowering; (3) accompanied, mastiff, pullets; (4) impertinent; (6) droll, kennel; (9) migration; (10) unfledged; (12) disconcerted.

# LESSON XXXIV (34)

## *Bonaparte Crossing the Alps*—SCOTT

RULE—Read this piece just as you think the person who wrote it would have spoken it. The reading must be adapted to the subject.

"Is this route practicable?" asked Bonaparte.

"It is barely possible to pass," replied the engineer.

"Let us set forward, then," said Napoleon, and the extraordinary march was commenced.

Bonaparte himself, on the 15th of May, at the head of the main body of his army, consisting of thirty thousand men and upwards, marched from Lausanne to the little village called St. Pierre, at which point there ended everything resembling a practicable road. An immense and apparently inaccessible mountain reared its head among general desolation and eternal frost. Precipices, glaciers, ravines, and a boundless extent of faithless snows, which the slightest concussion of the air converts into avalanches capable of burying armies in their descent, appeared to forbid access to all living things but the chamois and his scarcely less wild pursuer.

Yet, foot by foot and man by man did the French soldiers proceed to ascend this formidable barrier which Nature had erected in vain to limit human ambition. The view of the valley, emphatically called "Desolation," where nothing is to be seen but snow and sky, had no terrors for the First Consul and his army.

With the infantry loaded with arms and in full military equipment, they advanced by paths, until now, pursued only by hunters or here and there a hardy pedestrian. The cavalry leading their horses, the music of bands playing from time to time at the head of the regiments, and, in places of unusual difficulty, the drums beat a charge, as if to encourage the soldiers to encounter the opposition of Nature itself.

The pieces of artillery, without which they could not have done service, were deposited in trunks of trees hollowed out for the purpose. Each was dragged by a hundred men, and the troops, making it a point of honor to bring forward their guns, accomplished the severe duty, not with cheerfulness only, but with enthusiasm.

The carriages were taken to pieces and harnessed on the backs of mules or committed to the soldiers, who relieved each other in the task of bearing them with levers. The ammunition was transported in the same manner. While one half of the soldiers were thus engaged, the others were obliged to carry the muskets, cartridge boxes, knapsacks, and provisions of their comrades, as well as their own.

Each man, so loaded, was calculated to carry from sixty to seventy pounds weight up icy precipices where a man totally without encumbrance could ascend but slowly. Probably no troops, save the French, could have endured the fatigue of such a march, and no other general than Bonaparte would have ventured to require it at their hands.

Napoleon set out a considerable time after the march had begun, alone, excepting his guide. He is described by the Swiss peasant who attended him in that capacity, as wearing his usual simple dress, a gray overcoat and a three-cornered hat. He traveled in silence, save a few short and hasty questions about the country, addressed to his guide from time to time. When these were answered, he relapsed into silence.

There was a gloom on his brow, corresponding to the weather, which was wet and dismal. His countenance had acquired during his Eastern campaigns a swarthy complexion which, added to his natural severe gravity, inspired his Swiss guide with fear as he looked upon him. Occasionally his route was stopped by some temporary obstacle causing a halt in the artillery or baggage. His commands on such occasions were peremptorily given and instantly obeyed, his very look seeming enough to silence all objection and remove every difficulty. Above them they beheld everlasting snow; below them were the clouds.

The descent on the other side of Mont St. Bernard was as difficult to the infantry as the ascent had been, and still more so to the cavalry. It was, however, accomplished without material loss, and the army took up their quarters for the night, after having marched fourteen French leagues. The next morning, the 16th of May, the vanguard took possession of Aosta, a village of Piedmont, from which extends the valley of the same name, watered by the river Dorea, a country pleasant in itself, but rendered delightful by its contrast with the horrors which had been left behind.

QUESTIONS — 1. Why was Napoleon Bonaparte's crossing of the Alps so difficult? 2. What was Napoleon's mood as he followed his army? 3. How long did the crossing take and how far was it?

SPELL AND DEFINE — (4) precipices, glaciers, ravines; (5) formidable, Consul; (6) pedestrian; (8) knapsacks; (9) encumbrance; (10) relapsed; (11) corresponding; (12) vanguard.

# LESSON XXXV (35)

## *The Boy and the Butterfly*
### MRS. WILSON

RULE—In reading poetry be careful not to read too fast, and avoid the sing-song tone so common among learners.

Truant boy! with laughing eye
Chasing the winged butterfly
In her flight from bud to flower,
Wasting many a precious hour;
Thine's a chase of idle joy,
Happy, thoughtless, truant boy!

Thou hast left thy playmates, laid
'Neath the beech tree's leafy shade,
Sheltered from the hour of noon
And the burning skies of June;
What are hours or skies to thee,
Joyous type of liberty?

Pause!—Thy foot hath touch'd the brink,
Where the water lilies drink
Moisture from the silent stream,
Glittering in the sunny beam;
Truant, pause! or else the wave
May thy future idling save!

Now! pursue the painted thing!
See! she drops her velvet wing!
Tired, she rests on yonder rose,
Soon thy eager chase will close!
Stretch thine hand!—she is thine own!—
Ah!—she flies—thy treasure's gone!—

Boy! in thee the Poet's eye
Man's true emblem may descry;
Like thee, through the viewless air
He doth follow visions fair!
Hopes as vain—pursuits as wild,
Occupy the full-grown child!

QUESTIONS — 1. What is the boy in this poem doing? 2. Why is the word *truant* a good word to describe this boy? 3. Does the poetess condemn the boy?

# LESSON XXXVI (36)

## *The Goodness of God*—PSALM CIV

RULE—In reading such lessons as the following, be careful to read slowly and with great deliberation and seriousness. When sentences are short, and yet contain a great deal of meaning, you must allow the listener a little time to gather the sense and to dwell upon it.

1. Bless the Lord, O my soul! O Lord my God! thou art very great; thou art clothed with honor and majesty.

2. Who coverest thyself with light as with a garment; who stretchest out the heavens like a curtain.

3. Who layeth the beams of his chambers in the waters; who maketh the clouds his chariot; who walketh upon the wings of the wind:

4. Who maketh his angels spirits; his ministers a flaming fire:

5. Who laid the foundations of the earth, that it should not be removed forever.

6. Thou coveredst it with the deep as with a garment, the waters stood above the mountains.

7. At thy rebuke they fled; at the voice of thy thunder they hasted away.

8. They go up by the mountains; they go down by the valley unto the place which thou hast founded for them.

9. Thou hast set a bound that they may not pass over; that they turn not again to cover the earth.

10. He sendeth the springs into the valleys, which run among the hills.

11. They give drink to every beast of the field; the wild donkeys quench their thirst.

12. By them shall the fowls of the heaven have their habitation, which sing among the branches.

13. He watereth the hills from his chambers; the earth is satisfied with the fruit of thy works.

14. He causeth the grass to grow for the cattle, and herb for the service of man, that he may bring forth food out of the earth;

15. And wine that maketh glad the heart of man, and oil to make his face to shine, and bread which strengtheneth man's heart.

16. The trees of the Lord are full of sap; the cedars of Lebanon, which he hath planted;

17. Where the birds make their nests; as for the stork, the fir-trees are her house.

18. The high hills are a refuge for the wild goats, and the rocks for the conies.

19. He appointed the moon for seasons; the sun knoweth his going down.

20. Thou makest darkness, and it is night: wherein all the beasts of the forest do creep forth.

21. The young lions roar after their prey and seek their meat from God.

22. The sun ariseth, they gather themselves together, and lay them down in their dens.

23. Man goeth forth unto his work and to his labor until the evening.

24. O Lord, how manifold are thy works! in wisdom hast thou made them all. The earth is full of thy riches.

25. So is this great and wide sea, wherein are things creeping innumerable, both small and great beasts.

26. There go the ships; there is that leviathan, whom thou hast made to play therein.

27. These wait all upon thee, that thou mayest give them their meat in due season.

28. That thou givest them they gather: thou openest thine hand—they are filled with good.

29. Thou hidest thy face—they are troubled: thou takest away their breath—they die, and return to their dust.

30. Thou sendest forth thy spirit—they are created: and thou renewest the face of the earth.

31. The glory of the Lord shall endure forever: the Lord shall rejoice in his works.

32. He looketh on the earth—and it trembleth: he toucheth the hills—and they smoke.

QUESTIONS — This psalm reveals the character of God by stating some of the things He does. Select three verses that you like best and copy them on a sheet of paper. Be prepared to tell why you chose each of them.

SPELL AND DEFINE — (8) founded; (12) habitation; (18) refuge; (19) appointed; (25) innumerable; (26) leviathan.

# LESSON XXXVII (37)

## *Gospel Invitation*—ISAIAH LV

RULE—In reading the various names of the Supreme Being, great care should be taken to pronounce them distinctly and with reverence, but the custom of giving them an unnatural and drawling pronunciation must be always avoided.

1. Ho, everyone that thirsteth, come ye to the waters, and he that hath no money; come ye, buy and eat; yea, come, buy wine and milk, without money and without price.

2. Wherefore do ye spend money for that which is not bread? and your labor for that which satisfieth not? Hearken diligently unto me, and eat ye that which is good, and let your soul delight itself in fatness.

3. Incline your ear, and come unto me. Hear, and your soul shall live; and I will make an everlasting covenant with you, even the sure mercies of David.

4. Behold, I have given him for a witness to the people, a leader and commander to the people.

5. Behold, thou shalt call a nation that thou knowest not, and nations that knew not thee shall run unto thee, because of the Lord thy God, and for the Holy One of Israel; for he hath glorified thee.

6. Seek ye the Lord while he may be found, call upon him while he is near.

7. Let the wicked forsake his way, and the unrighteous man his thoughts; and let him return unto the Lord, and he will have mercy upon him; and to our God, for he will abundantly pardon.

8. For my thoughts are not your thoughts, neither are your ways my ways, saith the Lord.

9. For as the heavens are higher than the earth, so are my ways higher than your ways, and my thoughts than your thoughts.

10. For as the rain cometh down, and the snow from heaven, and returneth not thither, but watereth the earth, and maketh it bring forth and bud that it may give seed to the sower, and bread to the eater:

11. So shall my word be that goeth forth out of my mouth. It shall not return unto me void, but it shall accomplish that which I please, and it shall prosper in the thing whereto I sent it.

12. For ye shall go out with joy, and be led forth with peace: the mountains and the hills shall break forth before you into singing, and all the trees of the field shall clap their hands.

13. Instead of the thorn shall come up the fir-tree; and instead of the briar shall come up the myrtle-tree; and it shall be to the Lord for a name, for an everlasting sign that shall not be cut off.

QUESTIONS — 1. The four Gospels are located in the New Testament; Isaiah is a major book of the Old Testament. Why do you suppose McGuffey titled Isaiah 55, "Gospel Invitation?" 2. What are people told to do in verse six? 3. Read verse 11. What are some things that God's word accomplishes when people read or hear it?

SPELL AND DEFINE — (2) satisfieth; (3) everlasting, covenant; (4) commander; (7) unrighteous, abundantly; (11) void, accomplish.

# LESSON XXXVIII (38)

## *Works of the Coral*
## UNIVERSITY REVIEW

RULE—When you have finished reading a lesson, consider what you have learned from it before you begin another.

The coral varies in size from less than one inch to as much as one foot, a size attained by only a small percentage. It is by the persevering efforts of creatures so insignificant, working in myriads and working through ages, that the enormous structures in question are erected.

Enormous we may call them, when the Great Barrier Reef of Australia alone is a thousand miles in length and when its altitude, though yet scarcely fathomed in twenty places, cannot range to less than between one and two thousand feet. It is a mountain ridge that would reach almost three times from one extreme of England to the other, with the height of Ingleborough, or that of the ordinary and prevailing class of the Scottish mountains. And this is the work of animals whose dimensions are less than those of a housefly. It is perfectly overwhelming!

But what is even this? The whole of the Pacific Ocean is crowded with islands of the same architecture, the production of the same insignificant architects. An animal, barely possessing life, scarcely appearing to possess volition, tied down to its narrow cell, ephemeral in existence, is daily, hourly, creating the habitations of men, of animals, and of plants. It is founding a new continent; it is constructing a new world.

These are among the wonders of God's mighty

hand. Such are among the means which He uses to forward His ends of benevolence. Yet man, vain man, pretends to look down on the myriads of beings equally insignificant in appearance because he has not yet discovered the great offices which they hold, the duties which they fulfill in the great order of nature.

If we have said that coral is creating a new continent, we have not said more than the truth. Navigators now know that the great Southern Ocean is not only crowded with these islands, but that it is crowded with submarine rocks of the same nature, rapidly growing up to the surface, where, at length, overtopping the ocean, they are destined to form new habitations for man to extend his dominion.

They grow and unite into circles and ridges and ultimately, they become extensive tracts. This process cannot cease while those animals exist and propagate. It must increase in an accelerating ratio, and the result will be that, by the wider union of such islands, an extensive archipelago and at length a continent must be formed.

This process is equally visible in the Red Sea. It is daily becoming less and less navigable in consequence of the growth of its coral rocks. And the day may come when, perhaps, one plain will unite the opposite shores of Egypt and Arabia.

But let us here also admire the wonderful provision which is made deep in the earth for completing the work which those animals have commenced. And we may here note the contrast between the silent and unmarked labors of working myriads, operating by a universal and long ordained law, and the sudden, the momentary, effort of a power which, from the rarity of its exertions, seems to be especially among the miraculous interpositions of the Creator.

They are the volcano and the earthquake that are to complete the structure which the coral insect has laid, to elevate the mountain and to form the valley; to introduce beneath the equator the range of climate which belongs to the temperate regions, and to form the great hydraulic engine, by which the clouds are collected to water the earth, which causes the springs to burst forth and the rivers to flow.

And this is the work of one short hour. If the coral animals were not made in vain, neither was it for destruction that God ordained the volcano and the earthquake. Thus, also, by means so opposed, so contrasted, is one single end attained. And that end is the welfare, the happiness of man.

Man has but recently opened his eyes on the important facts which we have not stated, and his science is still unable to explain them.

QUESTIONS — 1. Describe the Great Barrier Reef of Australia. 2. How does the small coral create such enormous structures? 3. What benefits to mankind are the result of the work of the coral? The dangers?

SPELL AND DEFINE — (1) insignificant, myriads; (2) altitude, fathomed; (3) architecture, volition, ephemeral, continent; (5) navigators, submarine; (6) accelerating, archipelago; (8) interpositions.

# LESSON XXXIX (39)

## *The Coral*—MRS. SIGOURNEY

RULE—Be careful to pause wherever the sense or the measure requires it.

Toil on! toil on! ye ephemeral train,
Who build in the tossing and treacherous main;
Toil on—for the wisdom of man ye mock,
With your sand-based structures and domes of rock;
Your columns the fathomless fountains lave,
And your arches spring up to the crested wave;
You're a puny race, thus to boldly rear
A fabric so vast, in a realm so drear.

Ye bind the deep with your secret zone,
The ocean is sealed, and the surge a stone;
Fresh wreaths from the coral pavement spring,
Like the terraced pride of Assyria's king;
The turf looks green where the breakers rolled;
O'er the whirlpool ripens the ring of gold;
The sea-snatched isle is the home of men,
And mountains exult where the wave hath been.

But why do ye plant 'neath the billow dark
The wrecking reef for the gallant bark?
There are snares enough on the tented field,
'Mid the blossoming sweets that the valleys yield;
There are serpents to coil, ere the flowers are up;
There's a poison drop in man's purest cup;
There are foes that watch for his cradle breath,
And why need ye sow the floods with death?

With mouldering bones the deeps are white,
From the ice-clad pole to the tropics bright—

The mermaid hath twisted her fingers cold,
With the mesh of the sea-boy's curls of gold,
And the gods of the ocean have frowned to see
The mariner's bed in their halls of glee;—
Hath earth no graves, that ye thus must spread
The boundless sea for the thronging dead?

Ye build—ye build—but ye enter not in,
Like the tribes whom the desert devoured in their sin;
From the land of promise ye fade and die,
Ere its verdure gleams forth on your weary eye,—
As the kings of the cloud-crowned pyramid,
Their noteless bones in oblivion hid,
Ye slumber unmarked 'mid the desolate main,
While the wonder and pride of your works remain.

QUESTIONS — 1. In stanza one, for what does the poetess admire the coral? 2. In stanza three, the first two lines, the poet asks the coral a question. Re-word the question in your own words, so that its meaning is clear to you. 3. The poetess is speaking symbolically when she says, "There's a poison drop in man's purest cup." What does she mean? 4. From the last stanza quote two lines that show that the work of the coral endures after they die.

SPELL AND DEFINE — (3) billow, wrecking, reef, blossoming; (4) tropics, mermaid, mariner; (5) pyramid, oblivion.

# LESSON XL (40)

## *Value of Time and Knowledge*—HAWES

RULE—Read with care, but not with formality.

Let me call your attention to the importance of improving your time. The infinite value of time is not realized. It is the most precious thing in all the world—"the only thing of which it is a virtue to be covetous, and yet the only thing of which all men are prodigal."

In the first place, then, reading is a most interesting and pleasant method of occupying your leisure hours. All young people have, or may have, time enough to read. The difficulty is, they are not careful to improve it.

Their hours of leisure are either idled away, or talked away, or spent in some other way equally vain and useless. And then they complain that they have not time for the cultivation of their minds and hearts.

Time is so precious that there is never but one moment in the world at once, and that is always taken away before another is given. Only take care to gather up the fragments of time, and you will never want leisure for the reading of useful books. And in what way can you spend your unoccupied hours more pleasantly than in holding converse with the wise and the good through the medium of their writings! To a mind not altogether devoid of curiosity, books form an inexhaustible source of enjoyment.

It is a consideration of no small weight that reading furnishes materials for interesting and useful conversation. Those who are ignorant of books must, of course, have their thoughts confined to very narrow limits. What occurs in their immediate neighborhood, the state of the market, the idle report, the tale of scandal, the foolish story—these make up the circle of their knowledge and furnish the topics of their conversation. They have nothing to *say* of importance because they *know* nothing of importance.

A taste for useful reading is an effectual preservative from vice. Next to the fear of God implanted in the heart, nothing is a better safeguard to character than the love of *good* books. They are the handmaids of virtue and religion. They quicken our sense of duty, unfold our responsibilities, strengthen our principles, confirm our habits, inspire us in the love of what is right and useful, and teach us to look with disgust upon that which is low and groveling and vicious.

The high value of mental cultivation is another weighty motive for giving attendance to reading. What is it that mainly distinguishes a man from a brute? Knowledge. What makes the vast differences there is between savage and civilized nations? Knowledge. What forms the principal difference between men as they appear in the same society? Knowledge.

What raised Franklin from the humble station of a printer's boy to the first honors of his country? Knowledge. What took Sherman from his shoemaker's bench, gave him a seat in Congress and there made his voice to be heard among the wisest and best of his compeers? Knowledge. What raised Simpson from the weaver's loom to a place among the first of mathematicians; and Herschel, from being a poor fifer's boy in the army, to a station among the first of astronomers? Knowledge.

Knowledge is power. It is the philosopher's

stone—the true alchemy that turns everything it touches into gold. It is the scepter that gives us our dominion over nature, the key that unlocks the storehouse of creation and opens to us the treasures of the universe.

The circumstances in which you are placed, as the members of a free and intelligent community, demand of you a careful improvement of the means of knowledge you enjoy. You live in an age of great mental excitement. The public mind is awake, and society in general is fast rising on the scale of improvement. At the same time the means of knowledge are most abundant.

The road to wealth, to honor, to usefulness, and happiness is open to all, and all who will, may enter upon it with the almost certain prospect of success. In this free community there are no privileged orders. Every man finds his level. If he has talents, he will be known and estimated and rise in the respect and confidence of society.

Added to this, every man is here a freeman. He has a voice in the election of rulers, in making and executing the laws, and may be called to fill important places of honor and trust in the community of which he is a member. What then is the duty of persons in these circumstances? Are they not called to cultivate their minds, to improve their talents, and to acquire the knowledge which is necessary to enable them to act with honor and usefulness, the part assigned them on the stage of life.

A diligent use of the means of knowledge accords well with your nature as rational beings with the potential for eternal life. God has given you minds which are capable of indefinite improvement. He has placed you in circumstances peculiarly favorable for making such improvement. And to inspire you with diligence in mounting up the shining course before you, He points you to the prospect of an endless existence with Him.

If you have minds which are capable of endless progression in knowledge, of endless approximation to the supreme intelligence; if in the midst of unremitting success, objects of new interest will be forever opening before you—Oh what prospects are presented to the view of man! What strong inducements to cultivate his mind and heart and to enter upon that course of improvement here which is to run on, brightening in glory and in bliss, ages without end!

QUESTIONS — 1. What does the word prodigal mean in the phrase, ". . . the only thing of which all men are prodigal"? 2. Why is the reading of good books an important activity for leisure time? 3. In what ways do you waste time? How can you improve your use of time? 4. Identify by their accomplishments the people mentioned in paragraph 8. (Use a reference book.)

SPELL AND DEFINE — (4) unoccupied, inexhaustible; (5) consideration; (6) preservative, responsibilities; (7) cultivation; (8) congress, mathematicians; (9) philosopher; (14) progression, approximation.

# LESSON XLI (41)

## *Mountains, Lakes and Rivers*
### BRIT. NAT.

RULE—Read with moderation, neither too fast nor too slow. Rapid reading confounds all meaning and makes the sentences a mass of unintelligible sounds.

Mountains, lakes, and rivers are closely connected in the purposes they serve in the economy of nature, and are each (especially the last) of great importance to man. The mountain is the father of streams, and the lake is the regulator of their discharge. The lofty summit of the mountain attracts and breaks the clouds, which would otherwise pass over without falling to water the earth.

This moisture is collected in snow and laid up in a store against the bleak drought of spring; and as the water into which the melting snow is gradually converted during the thaw, penetrates deep into the fissures of the rock or into the porous strata of loose materials, the fountains continue to pour out their cooling stores during the summer.

The lake, as has been mentioned, prevents the waste of water which would otherwise take place in mountain-rivers, as well as the ravage and ruin by which that waste would be attended.

But though mountains and lakes have thus their beauty and their value, they cannot, in either respect, be compared to the river. They are fixed in their places, but the river is continually in motion—the emblem of life—the active servant of man—and one of the greatest means of communication and, consequently, of civilization.

The spots where man first put forth his powers as a rational being were on the banks of rivers. If no Euphrates had rolled its waters to the Indian Ocean, and no Nile its flood to the Mediterranean, the learning of the Chaldeans and the wisdom of the Egyptians would never have shone forth; and the western world, which is indebted to them for the rudiments of science and the spirit which leads to the cultivation of science, might still have been in a state of ignorance and barbarity, no way superior to that of the nations of Australia, where the want of rivers separates the people into little hordes and prevents that general communication which is essential to even a very moderate degree of civilization.

Nor ought we to omit to mention that the river is a minister of health and purity. It carries off the superabundant moisture which, if left to stagnate on the ground, would be injurious both to plants and animals. It carries off to the sea those saline products, which result from animal and vegetable decomposition and which soon convert into deserts, those places where there are no streams.

QUESTIONS — 1. How are mountains, lakes and rivers interrelated in their ecological work? 2. How does a river contribute to knowledge and civilization? 3. When was Australia settled by Europeans? What is the Australian culture like today?

SPELL AND DEFINE — (1) economy; (2) drought, strata, fissures; (4) civilization; (5) rudiments; (6) superabundant.

# LESSON XLII (42)

## *Character of Martin Luther*
### ROBERTSON

RULE—The little word *and* is very improperly pronounced, as if it were written *und* or *an*.

Luther was raised up by Providence to be the author of one of the greatest and most interesting revolutions recorded in history, and there is no person, perhaps, whose character has been drawn with such opposite colors. Some were struck with horror and inflamed with rage when they saw with what a daring hand he overturned everything which they held to be sacred or valued as beneficial, and imputed to him not only all the defects and vices of a man, but also the qualities of a demon.

Others were warmed with the admiration and gratitude which they thought he merited as the restorer of light and liberty to the Christian church. They ascribed to him perfections above the condition of humanity and viewed all his actions with a veneration bordering on that which should be paid only to those who are guided by the immediate inspiration of Heaven. It is his own conduct, not the distinguishing censure or the exaggerated praise of his contemporaries, that ought to regulate the opinions of the present age concerning him.

Zeal for what he regarded as truth, undaunted intrepidity to maintain his own system, abilities both natural and acquired to defend his principles, and unwearied industry in propagating them are virtues which shine so conspicuously in every part of his behavior that even his enemies must allow him to have possessed them in an eminent degree.

To these may be added with equal justice, such purity of manners as became one who assumed the character of a reformer, such sanctity of life as suited the doctrine which he delivered, and such perfect disinterestedness as affords no slight presumption of his sincerity.

His extraordinary qualities were alloyed with not inconsiderable mixture of human frailty and human passions. These, however, were of such a nature that they cannot be imputed to malevolence or corruption of heart, but seem to have taken their rise from the same source with many of his virtues. His mind, forcible and vehement in all its operations, roused by great objects or agitated by violent passions, broke out on many occasions with an impetuosity which astonished men of feebler spirits, or such as are placed in a more tranquil situation.

By carrying some praiseworthy dispositions to excess, he bordered sometimes on what was culpable and was often betrayed into actions which exposed him to censure. His confidence that his own opinions were well founded approached to arrogance; his courage in asserting them, to rashness; his firmness in adhering to them, to obstinacy; and his zeal in confuting his adversaries, to rage and scurrility.

Accustomed, himself, to consider everything as subordinate to truth, he expected the same deference for it from other men, and without making any allowances for their timidity or prejudices, he poured forth against such as disappointed him on the particular point, a torrent of invective mingled with contempt.

But these indecencies of which Luther was guilty, must not be imputed wholly to the violence of his temper. In passing judgment upon the characters of men, we ought to try them by the principles and maxims of their own age, not by those of another; for, although virtue and vice are at all times the same, manners and customs continually vary.

Some parts of Luther's behavior, which to us appears most culpable, gave no disgust to his contemporaries. It was even by some of those qualities, which we are now apt to blame, that he was fitted for accomplishing the great work which he undertook. To raise mankind when sunk in ignorance and superstition and to encounter the rage of bigotry, armed with power, required the utmost vehemence of zeal, as well as a temper daring to excess.

A gentle call would neither have reached nor have excited those to whom it must have been addressed. A spirit more amiable, but less vigorous than Luther's, would have shrunk back from the dangers which he braved and surmounted. Towards the close of Luther's life, though without any perceptible diminution of his zeal or abilities, the infirmities of his temper increased upon him so that he grew daily more peevish, more irascible, and more impatient of contradiction.

Having lived to be a witness of his own amazing success, to see a great part of Europe embrace his doctrine, and to shake the foundation of the papal throne, before which the mightiest monarch has trembled, he discovered, on some occasions, symptoms of vanity and self-applause. He must have been, indeed, more than man, if, upon contemplating all that he actually accomplished, he had never felt any sentiment of this kind rising in his breast.

Some time before his death (which took place in 1546), he felt his strength declining, his constitution being worn out by a prodigious multiplicity of business, added to the labor of discharging his ministerial function with unremitting diligence, to the fatigue of constant study, besides the composition of works as voluminous as if he had enjoyed uninterrupted leisure and retirement.

His natural intrepidity did not forsake him at the approach of death. His last conversation with his friends was concerning the happiness reserved for good men in future life, of which he spoke with the fervor and delight natural to one who expected and wished to enter soon upon the enjoyment of it.

The account of his death filled the Roman Catholic party with excessive as well as indecent joy and damped the spirits of all his followers. Neither party sufficiently considered that his doctrines were now so firmly rooted as to be in a condition to flourish independently of the hand which first planted them. His funeral was celebrated by order of the Elector of Saxony with extraordinary pomp.

QUESTIONS — 1. The writer of this lesson assumes that you already know the chief accomplishments of Martin Luther. Do you? If not, use an encyclopedia to find out what those accomplishments were. 2. According to the writer, what were some character flaws of Martin Luther? 3. Why does every human being—regardless of his/her accomplishments—have character flaws?

SPELL AND DEFINE — (1) Providence, revolutions; (2) contemporaries; (3) propagating; (4) disinterestedness; (5) malevolence; (6) confuting; (7) subordinate; (9) accomplishing; (10) irascible; (12) multiplicity; (13) intrepidity.

# LESSON XLIII (43)

## *The Importance of Well-Spent Youth*

RULE—It is a poor excuse for an error, to say, "I had forgotten"; therefore, in this lesson bear in mind the preceding rules.

As the beauty of summer, the fruitfulness of autumn, and the support of winter depends upon spring, so the happiness, wisdom, and piety of middle life and old age depend upon youth. Youth is the seed time of life.

If the farmer does not plow his land and commit the precious seed to the ground in spring, it will be too late afterwards; so if we, while young, neglect to cultivate our hearts and minds by not sowing the seeds of knowledge and virtue, our future lives will be ignorant, vicious, and wretched. "The sluggard will not plow by reason of the cold. He, therefore, shall beg in harvest and have nothing."

The soil of the human heart is naturally barren of everything good, though prolific of evil. If corn, flowers, or trees are not planted and carefully cultivated, nettles and brambles will spring up; and the mind, if not cultivated and stored with useful knowledge, will become a barren desert or a thorny wilderness.

"I went by the field of the slothful and by the vineyard of the man void of understanding, and lo, it was all grown over with thorns, and nettles had covered the face thereof, and the stone wall thereof was broken down." When our first parents had sinned, the ground was cursed for their sake, and God said, "Thorns also and thistles shall it bring forth," but this curse is turned into a blessing by the diligent and industrious, who are never happy when unemployed, who delight in labor and exertion and receive an ample reward for all their toils.

As the spring is the most important part of the year, so is youth the most important period of life. Surely God has a claim to our first and principal attention, and religion demands the morning of our days, and the first season, the spring of our lives. Before we are encumbered by cares, distressed by afflictions, or engaged in business, it becomes us to resign our souls to God.

Perhaps you may live for many years; then you will be happy in possessing knowledge and piety and be enabled to do good to others. If, just as youth is showing its buds and blossoms, the flower should be snapped from its stalk by the rude hand of death, O how important that it should be transplanted from earth, to flourish forever at the foot of the tree of life and beside the waters of the river of life in heaven!

QUESTIONS — 1. What analogy is used in this lesson? (If you are unfamiliar with the word *analogy*, check your dictionary.) 2. Talk individually with two adults whom you admire for their Christian character and ask each of them what some of the important decisions of their youth were.

SPELL AND DEFINE — (1) fruitfulness; (2) sluggard; (4) vineyard; (5) encumbered; (6) possessing, transplanted.

# LESSON XLIV (44)

## *The Old Oaken Bucket*—WOODWORTH

RULE—There is a large class of words beginning with *pre*, such as *present, predict,* and *prevent,* which are pronounced as if they were written, *pr-sent, pr-dict, pr-vent.* This is to be carefully avoided.

How dear to my heart
     are the scenes of my childhood,
  When fond recollection presents them to view!
The orchard, the meadow,
     the deep tangled wildwood,
  And every loved spot which my infancy knew;
The wide spreading pond,
     and the mill which stood by it;
  The bridge, and the rock where the cataract fell;
The cot of my father, the dairy house nigh it,
     And even the rude bucket
     which hung in the well!
The old oaken bucket, the iron-bound bucket,
    The moss-covered bucket,
      which hung in the well.


That moss-covered vessel I hail as a treasure;
  For often, at noon, when returned from the field,
I found it the source of an exquisite pleasure,
  The purest and sweetest that nature can yield.
How ardent I seized it,
     with hands that were glowing,
  And quick to the white pebbled bottom it fell;
Then soon, with the emblem of truth overflowing,
    And dripping with coolness,
     it rose from the well:
The old oaken bucket, the iron-bound bucket,
    The moss-covered bucket arose from the well.

How sweet from the green mossy brim
    to receive it,
  As poised on the curb it inclined to my lips!
Not a full blushing goblet
    could tempt me to leave it,
  Though filled with the nectar that Jupiter sips.
And now, far removed from thy loved situation,
  The tear of regret will intrusively swell,
As fancy reverts to my father's plantation,
  And sighs for the bucket
    which hangs in the well;
The old oaken bucket, the iron-bound bucket,
  The moss-covered bucket,
    which hangs in the well.

QUESTIONS — 1. This poem is included in a book entitled, *Best Loved Poems of the American People*. Why do you think it is? 2. Notice the last two lines of each stanza. How are they the same and how are they different? 3. When you become an adult and think back to the days of your childhood, what scenes do you suppose you will treasure? On a sheet of paper write the first line of this poem: "How dear to my heart are the scenes of my childhood." Then, under it, list scenes *you* will treasure. Start each new scene on a new line. Do not try to rhyme the end words. With a little coaching from an adult, you could refine your ideas into a very pleasant, unrhymed poem.

SPELL AND DEFINE — (1) infancy; (2) treasure; (3) poised, intrusively.

# LESSON XLV (45)

## *The Giraffe*

RULE—Whenever you meet with a parenthesis in reading, read it in a softer and lower tone than you do the other parts of the sentence.

The giraffe is a native of Africa. It is of singular shape and size and bears some resemblance both to the camel and the deer. The mouth is small, the eyes full and brilliant, the tongue is rough, very long, and terminates in a point. The neck is extremely long and slender, and from the shoulder to the top of the head, it measures between seven and eight feet. From the ground to the top of the shoulder is commonly ten or eleven feet, so that the height of a full grown giraffe is seventeen or eighteen feet.

The hair is of a deep brown color in the male and of a light or yellowish brown in the female. The skin is beautifully diversified with white spots. They have short, obtuse horns, and hoofs resembling those of the ox. In their wild state, they feed on the leaves of a species of the mimosa, a gum-bearing tree peculiar to warm climates.

The giraffe (like the horse and other hoofed animals) defends itself by kicking. Its hinder limbs are so light and its blows so rapid that the eye cannot follow them. They are sufficient for its defense against the lion. It never employs its horns in resisting the attack of an enemy. Its disposition is gentle, and it flees to its native forest upon the least alarm.

La Vaillant, the celebrated French traveler and naturalist, was the first who gave us any precise account of the form and habits of the giraffe. While he was traveling in South Africa, he happened one day to discover a hut covered with the skin of one of those animals and learned, to his surprise, that he was now in a part of the country which the creature inhabited. He could not rest contented until he had seen the animal alive and secured a specimen.

Having on several successive days obtained sight of some of them, he with his attendants on horseback and accompanied with dogs, gave chase, but they baffled all pursuit. After a chase of a whole day, which affected nothing but the fatigue of the party, he began to despair of success.

The next day, says he, "By sunrise I was in pursuit of game, in the hope of obtaining some provision for my men. After several hours' fatigue, we saw at the turn of a hill, seven giraffes, which my pack of dogs instantly pursued. Six of them went off together, but the seventh, cut off by my dogs, took another way.

"I followed the single one at full speed, but in spite of the efforts of my horse, she got so much ahead of me, that in turning a little hill I lost sight of her altogether, and I gave up the pursuit. My dogs, however, were not so easily exhausted. They were soon so close upon her that she was obliged to stop and defend herself. From the noise they made, I conjectured that they had got the animal into a corner, and again pushed forward.

"I had scarcely got round the hill, when I perceived her surrounded by the dogs and endeavoring to drive them away by heavy kicks. In a moment I was on my feet, and a shot from my carbine brought her to the earth. . . . I was transported with my victory. I was now able to add to the riches of natural history. I was now able to destroy the romance which attached to this animal and to establish the truth of its existence."

QUESTIONS — 1. Why did La Vaillant have a difficult time finding a giraffe? 2. Was La Vaillant's killing of the giraffe justified? Why or why not?

SPELL AND DEFINE — (1) brilliant; (2) diversified, peculiar; (4) naturalist, specimen; (5) fatigue; (8) carbine, romance.

# LESSON XLVI (46)

## Consider Both Sides of the Question

RULE—Some words in a sentence require much more stress of voice and more time in pronouncing them than others, and these words are called *emphatical*. We give emphasis, or force of pronunciation, to those words which are of the most importance in a sentence and to those which require such forcible utterance as shows that they are used with some peculiar meaning.

In the days of knight-errantry and paganism, one of the old British princes set up a statue to the goddess of Victory at a point where four roads met together. In her right hand she held a spear, and her left hand rested upon a shield. The outside of this shield was of gold and the inside of silver. On the former was inscribed in the old British language, "To the goddess ever favorable," and on the other, "For four victories obtained successively over the Picts and other inhabitants of the northern islands."

It happened one day that two knights completely armed, one in black armor, the other in white, arrived from the opposite parts of the country at the statue just about the same time. As neither of them had seen it before, they stopped to read the inscription and observe the excellence of its workmanship.

After contemplating it for some time, the black knight said, "This golden shield . . ."

"*Golden* shield!" cried the white knight, who was as strictly observing the opposite side, "Why, if I have my eyes, it is silver."

"I know nothing of your eyes," replied the black knight, "but if ever I saw a golden shield in my life, this is one."

"Yes," returned the white knight, smiling, "it is very probable, indeed, that they should expose a shield of gold in so public a place as this! For my part, I wonder even a silver one is not too strong a temptation for the honesty of some people who pass this way. It appears by the date that this has been here more than three years."

The black knight could not bear the smile with which this was delivered and grew so warm in the dispute, that it soon ended in a challenge. They both, therefore, turned their horses and rode back so far as to have sufficient space for their encounter. Then, fixing their spears in their rests, they flew at each other with the greatest fury and impetuosity. Their shock was so rude and the blow on each side so effectual that they both fell to the ground, much wounded and bruised and lay there for some time as in a trance.

A good Druid, who was traveling that way, found them in this condition. The Druids were the physicians of those times, as well as priests. With him he had a sovereign balsam, which he had compounded himself, for he was very skillful in all the plants that grew in the fields or in the forests. He stanched their blood, applied his balsam to their wounds, and brought them, as it were, from death to life again. As soon as they were sufficiently recovered, he began to inquire into the occasion of their quarrel. "Why, this man," cried the black knight, "will have it that yonder shield is silver."

"And he will have," replied the white knight, "that it is gold."

Then they told him all the particulars of the affair.

"Ah," said the Druid, with a sigh, "you are both, my brethren in the right, and both of you in the wrong. Had either of you given himself time to look at the opposite side of the shield, as well as that which first presented itself to view, all this passion and bloodshed might have been avoided. However, there is a very good lesson to be learned from the evils which have befallen you on this occasion. Permit me, therefore, to entreat you never to enter into any dispute for the future until you have fairly considered both sides of the question."

QUESTIONS — Draw a series of pictures to illustrate this story. If you wish, add the words spoken by the characters.

SPELL AND DEFINE — (1) paganism, inhabitants; (2) armor, statue, knights, inscription; (3) shield; (7) challenge, impetuosity; (8) Druid.

# LESSON XLVII (47)

## *Tomorrow*—COTTON

RULE—This lesson is written in blank verse, which is the most difficult of all kinds of composition to read well. It must not be read as if it were mere prose, for it has a measure, neither must it be read as other poetry, for its measure is not so regular and fixed. The reader who is learning, should perhaps attempt nothing further than a simple and clear expression of the sense.

Tomorrow! didst thou say?
Methought I heard Horatio say, Tomorrow.
Got to—I will not hear of it. —Tomorrow!
'Tis a sharper, who stakes his penury
Against thy plenty—who takes thy ready cash
And pays thee nought but wishes,
    hopes, and promises,
The currency of idiots. Injurious bankrupt,
That gulls the easy creditor! —Tomorrow!
It is a period nowhere to be found
In all the hoary register of time,
Unless perchance in the fool's calendar.
Wisdom disclaims the word, nor holds society
With those who own it. No, my Horatio,
'Tis Fancy's child, and Folly is its Father;
Wrought of such stuff as dreams are;
    and as baseless
As the fantastic visions of the evening.

But soft, my friend—arrest the
    present moments;
For be assured, they all are arrant tell-tales:
And though their flight be silent,
    and their pathway
Trackless as the winged couriers of the air,
They post to heaven and there record thy folly.

Because, though stationed on the
          important watch,
Thou, like a sleeping, faithless sentinel,
Didst let them pass unnoticed, unimproved;
And know, for that thou slumberedst
          on the guard,
Thou shalt be made to answer at the bar
For every fugitive: and when thou thus
Shalt stand impleaded at the high tribunal
Of lynx-eyed justice, who shall tell thy audit?

     Then stay the present instant, dear Horatio;
Imprint the mark of wisdom on its wings;
'Tis of more worth than kingdoms!
          far more precious
Than all the crimson treasures of life's fountain!
Oh! let it not elude thy grasp; but like
The good old patriarch upon record,
Hold the fleet angel fast until he bless thee.

QUESTIONS — 1. What is wrong with *tomorrow*, according to
the poet? 2. Instead of *tomorrow*, what should we treasure?
3. To whom is the poet alluding in the last three lines of the
poem?

SPELL AND DEFINE — penury, perchance, disclaims, base-
less, fantastic, trackless, couriers, impleaded, patriarch.

# LESSON XLVIII (48)

## *The Generous Russian Peasant*
### KARAMSIN

RULE—If you meet with difficult words or foreign names, do not fly over them, but read them distinctly.

Let Virgil sing the praises of Augustus, genius celebrate merit, and flattery extol the talents of the great. The short and simple "annals of the poor" engross my pen, and while I record the history of Flor Silin's virtues, though I speak of a poor peasant, I shall describe a noble man. I ask no eloquence to assist me in the task—modest worth rejects the aid of ornament to set it off.

It is impossible, even at this distant period, to reflect without horror, on the miseries of that year, known in Lower Volga by the name of the *famine year*. I remember the summer, whose scorching heats had dried up all the fields, and the drought had no relief but from the tears of the ruined farmer.

I remember the cold, comfortless autumn, and the despairing rustics, crowding round their empty farms with folded arms and sorrowful countenances, pondering on their misery instead of rejoicing, as usual, at the golden harvest. I remember the winter which succeeded, and I reflect with agony on the miseries it brought with it. Whole families left their homes to become beggars on the highway.

At night the canopy of heaven served them as their only shelter from the piercing winds and bitter frost. To describe these scenes would be to harm the feelings of my readers; therefore, to my tale. In those days, I lived on an estate not far from Simbirsk; and, though but a child, I have not forgotten the impression made on my mind by the general calamity.

In an adjoining village lived Flor Silin, a poor laboring peasant—a man remarkable for his assiduity and the skill and judgment with which he cultivated his lands. He was blessed with abundant crops; and his means being larger than his wants, his granaries, even at this time, were full of corn. The dry year coming on had beggared all the village except himself. Here was an opportunity to grow rich! Mark how Flor Silin acted. Having called the poorest of his neighbors about him, he addressed them in the following manner:

"My friends, you lack corn for your subsistence. God has blessed me with abundance. Assist in thrashing out a quantity, and each of you take what he wants for his family."

The peasants were amazed at this unexampled generosity, for sordid propensities exist in the village as well as in the populous city.

The fame of Flor Silin's benevolence having reached other villages, the famished inhabitants presented themselves before him and begged for corn. This good creature received them as brothers, and while his store remained, afforded all relief. At length his wife, seeing no end to the generosity of his noble spirit, reminded him how necessary it would be to think on their own wants and hold his lavish hand before it was too late. "It is written in the scripture," said he, "Give, and it shall be given unto you."

The following year Providence listened to the prayers of the poor, and the harvest was abundant. The peasants, who had been saved from starving by Flor Silin, now gathered around him.

"Behold," said they, "the corn you lent us. You saved our wives and children. We should have been famished but for you. May God reward you. He only can. All we have to give is our corn and grateful thanks."

"I lack no corn at present, my good neighbors," said he. "My harvest has exceeded all my expectations, for the rest, thank Heaven, I have been but an humble instrument."

They urged him in vain. "No," said he, "I shall not accept your corn. If you have surplus, share it among your poor neighbors, who, being unable to sow their fields last autumn, are still in want. Let us assist them, my dear friends. The Almighty will bless us for it."

"Yes," replied the grateful peasants, "our poor neighbors shall have this corn. They shall know that it is to you they owe this timely help and join to teach their children the debt of gratitude due to your benevolent heart."

Silin raised his tearful eyes to heaven. An angel might have envied him his feelings.

QUESTIONS — 1. What had caused the famine? 2. How did Flor Silin act towards his neighbors? 3. Instead of repaying him when they had an abundant crop, what did Flor Silin suggest that the farmers do with their grain? 4. For what might the angels have envied Flor Silin?

SPELL AND DEFINE — (1) annals; (4) canopy, estate; (5) assiduity, granaries; (7) propensities; (8) lavish; (9) harvest.

# LESSON XLIX (49)

## *The Winter King*—MISS GOULD

RULE—In this lesson there is a pause at the end of every line. In pieces where this is not the case, however, beware of attempting to *make* the rhymes jingle by improper stops.

O! what will become of thee, poor little bird!
The muttering storm in the distance is heard!
The rough winds are waking,
    the clouds growing black,
They'll soon scatter snowflakes all over thy back!
From what sunny clime hast thou wandered away,
And what art thou doing this cold winter day?

"I'm picking the gum from the old peach tree—
The storm doesn't trouble me! Tee, dee, dee."

But what makes thee seem
    so unconscious of care?
The brown earth is frozen, the branches are bare:
And how canst thou be so light-hearted and free,
As if danger and suffering
    thou never should'st see,
When no place is near for thy evening nest?
No leaf for thy screen, for thy bosom no rest?

"Because the same hand is a shelter for me,
That took off the summer leaves—Tee, dee, dee."

But man feels a burden of care and grief,
While plucking the cluster and binding the sheaf.
In the summer we faint,
    in the winter we're chilled,
With ever a void that is yet to be filled.

We take from the ocean, the earth, and the air,
Yet all their rich gifts do not silence our care.

"A very small portion sufficient will be,
If sweetened with gratitude! Tee, dee, dee."

I thank thee, bright monitor;
    what thou hast taught,
Will oft be the theme of the happiest thought;
*We* look at the *clouds*—
    while the *birds* have an eye
To *Him who reigns over them*,
    changeless and high.
And now, little hero, just tell me thy name,
That I may be sure whence my oracle came.

"Because in all weather I'm merry and free,
They call me the Winter King—Tee, dee, dee."

But soon there'll be ice
    weighing down the light bough
On which thou art flitting so playfully now;
And though there's a vesture
    well fitted and warm,
Protecting the rest of thy delicate form,
What, then, wilt thou do with thy little bare feet,
To save them from pain,
    'mid the frost and the sleet?

"I can draw them right up
    in my feathers, you see,
To warm them, and fly away! Tee, dee, dee."

QUESTIONS — 1. Unlike the bird in this poem, what attitude do people carry with them as they work? 2. What lesson has the bird taught the poetess? (See stanza seven.)

SPELL AND DEFINE — (1) muttering; (3) unconscious; (7) monitor.

# LESSON L (50)

## *Touch Not, Taste Not, Handle Not*

RULE—When there are poetical quotations in prose pieces, they should be read as if they were part of the same line, unless the sense requires a pause.

"Wine is a mocker, and strong drink is raging. Who hath woe? Who hath sorrow? Who hath contentions? Who hath babbling? Who hath wounds without a cause? Who hath redness of eyes? They that tarry long at the wine."

How often do men meet in good humor, then drink to excess, talk nonsense, fancy themselves insulted, take fire within, rave, threaten, and then come to blows? A long time ago, Seneca spoke of those who "let in a thief at the mouth to steal away the brains." In such a case the stupidity of a brute is often united with the fury of a demoniac. Nay, the man among the tombs was comparatively harmless; he only injured himself. But how often does the drunken revel end in the cry of murder!

How often does the hand of the intoxicated man, lifted against his dearest friend, perhaps the wife of his bosom, ". . . In one rash hour, Perform a deed that haunts him to the grave!"

Could I call around me, in one vast assembly, the young men of this nation, I would say: Hopes of my country, blessed be ye of the Lord, now in the dew of your youth. But look well to your footsteps, for vipers and scorpions and adders surround your way. Look at the generation who have just preceded you. The morning of their life was cloudless, and it dawned as brightly as your own. But behold now, the smitten, enfeebled, inflamed, debauched, idle, poor, irreligious, and vicious with halting step, dragging onward to meet an early grave.

Their bright prospects are clouded, and their sun is set never to rise. No house of their own receives them, while from poorer to poorer tenements they descend as improvidence dries up their resources. And, now, who are those that wait on their footsteps with muffled faces and sable garments? This is a father and that is a mother, whose gray hairs are coming with sorrow to the grave. That is a sister, weeping over evils which she cannot arrest; and there is the brokenhearted wife; and these are the children—hapless innocents—for whom their father has provided no inheritance, only one of dishonor and nakedness and woe!

And is this, beloved youth, the history of your course? In this scene of desolation do you see the image of your future selves? Is this the poverty and the disease which, as an armed man, shall take hold on you? And are your relatives and friends to succeed those who now move on in this mournful procession, weeping as they go?

Yes, bright as your morning now opens and high as your hopes beat, *this* is *your* noon and *your* night, unless you shun those habits of intemperance which have thus early made theirs a day of clouds and of thick darkness. If you frequent places of evening resort for social drinking, if you set out with drinking daily, a little, prudently, temperately, it is *yourselves* which, as in a glass, you behold.

"One of the greatest consolations afforded to my mind by the success of the temperance cause, is the reflection that my child will not be a drunkard." Such was the language of a distinguished philanthropist, as he held a listening assembly chained by the voice of his eloquence.

To this remark the heart of every parent assents;

for that the progress of the temperance cause will be so great, at the period when the child, which is now an infant, shall come upon the theater of life, as to render all use of ardent spirit, as a drink, disreputable, can scarce be questioned.

If any father or mother could lift the veil of the future and read on the page of coming years that the son, now so loved, so idolized perhaps, would become a bloated, polluted and polluting creature, reeling under the influence of ardent spirit, the remainder of life would be wretched. To such a parent, this world would indeed be a vale of tears and the silence and solitude of the tomb would be welcomed as the place where the weary might be at rest.

The temperance reform does in fact lift the veil of years and discloses to the parents of the present generation, their children and their children's children freed from all the woes and curses of drunkenness, the smile of gratitude upon their countenance, and the language of benediction upon their lips.

"My child will not be a drunkard!" Cheering thought! How it swells the heart with emotions too big for utterance! What an animating prospect does it open to the mind! Alms-houses and jails and penitentiaries and state prisons will then stand only as so many monuments of the vices of an age gone by, and the evils consequent upon the use of ardent spirit shall exist only upon the historian's page, as so many records of the former degeneracy and the errors of mankind.

QUESTIONS — 1. What are some of the troubles caused by drinking alcoholic beverages? 2. Besides the intemperate person, who else suffers because of his/her drinking problem? 3. This lesson was written during a time in the United States when there was a very active temperance movement. The writer was sure that the day would come (in your generation—now) when the evils caused by alcoholic beverage would be remembered only by the history books. What went wrong?

SPELL AND DEFINE — (1) contentions; (2) demoniac, comparatively; (3) intoxicated; (4) generation, inflamed; (5) inheritance; (6) desolation; (8) consolations, philanthropist; (11) reform; (12) alms-house, penitentiaries, monuments, degeneracy.

# LESSON LI (51)

## *The Voice of Nature*—PSALM XIX

RULE—When reading the sacred scriptures, employ such tones and such a manner as become a creature who is reading a revelation from the Creator.

1. The heavens declare the glory of God; and the firmament showeth his handiwork.

2. Day unto day uttereth speech, and night unto night showeth knowledge.

3. There is no speech nor language, where their voice is not heard.

4. Their line is gone out through all the earth, and their words to the end of the world. In them hath he set a tabernacle for the sun;

5. Which is as a bridegroom coming out of his chamber, and rejoiceth as a strong man to run a race.

6. His going forth is from the end of the heaven, and his circuit unto the ends of it: and there is nothing hid from the heat thereof.

7. The law of the Lord is perfect, converting the soul: the testimony of the Lord is sure, making wise the simple.

8. The statutes of the Lord are right, rejoicing the heart: the commandment of the Lord is pure, enlightening the eyes.

9. The fear of the Lord is clean, enduring forever; the judgments of the Lord are true and righteous altogether.

10. More to be desired are they than gold, yea, than much fine gold, sweeter also than honey and the honeycomb.

11. Moreover, by them is thy servant warned, and in keeping of them there is great reward.

12. Who can understand his errors: Cleanse Thou me from secret faults.

13. Keep back thy servant also from presumptuous sins: let them not have dominion over me; then shall I be upright, and I shall be innocent from the great transgression.

14. Let the words of my mouth, and the meditation of my heart, be acceptable in thy sight, O Lord, my Strength and my Redeemer.

QUESTIONS — This very beautiful and well-known Psalm praises two different ways to learn about God. 1. How is God revealed according to verses 1–6? 2. How is God revealed according to verses 7–11? 3. What is the Psalmist's attitude toward the word of the Lord? 4. In verses 7–11 find five synonyms that have been used in this Psalm for *word of the Lord.*

SPELL AND DEFINE — (1) firmament; (4) tabernacle; (13) presumptuous, dominion, transgression; (14) meditation, Redeemer.

# LESSON LII (52)

## *Ode From the 19th Psalm*—ADDISON

RULE—In reading poetry of this kind, a very slight pause may
be made at the end of the line where there is no printed stop.

The spacious firmament on high,
With all the blue ethereal sky,
And spangled heavens, a shining frame,
Their great Original proclaim.
The unwearied sun, from day to day,
Does his Creator's power display;
And publishes to every land
The work of an Almighty hand.

Soon as the evening shades prevail,
The moon takes up the wondrous tale,
And, nightly, to the listening earth,
Repeats the story of her birth;
Whilst all the stars that round her burn,
And all the planets in their turn,
Confirm the tidings as they roll,
And spread the truth from pole to pole.

What though in solemn silence, all
Move round the dark terrestrial ball;
What though no real voice nor sound
Amid these radiant orbs be found;
In *reason's* ear they all rejoice,
And utter forth a glorious voice,
Forever singing, as they shine,
"The Hand that made us is divine."

QUESTIONS — 1. Even though the sun, moon, and stars have
no voice, what do they forever sing? 2. What is the "dark terres-

trial ball"? (stanza three) 3. In the preceding lesson you read Psalm 19 from the King James Version. Point out differences and similarities between the Psalm and Addison's "Ode from the 19th Psalm."

# LESSON LIII (53)

## *The Festal Board*

RULE—When there is no point at the end of the line, though you are required to pause for sake of the measure, be careful not to let the voice fall, as where there is a full stop.

Come to the festal board tonight—
  For bright eyed beauty will be there,
Her coral lips in nectar steeped,
  And garlanded her hair.

Come to the festal board tonight—
  For there the joyous laugh of youth
Will ring those silvery peals, which speak
  Of bosoms pure, and stainless truth.

Come to the festal board tonight—
  For friendship, there, with stronger chain,
Devoted hearts already bound
  For good or ill, will bind again.
     *I went.*

Nature and art their stores outpoured;
  Joy beamed in every kindling glance;
Love, friendship, youth and beauty, smiled;
  What could that evening's bliss enhance?
     *We parted.*

And years have flown—but where are now
   The guests who round that table met?
Rises their sun as gloriously
   As on the banquet's eve it set?

How holds the chain which friendship wore?
   It broke; —and, soon, the hearts it bound
Were widely sundered; and for peace,
   Envy and strife and blood were found.

The merriest laugh which then was heard
   Has changed its tones to maniac screams,
As half-quenched memory kindles up
   Glimmerings of guilt in feverish dreams.

And where is she, whose diamond eyes
   Golconda's purest gems outshone—
Whose roseate lips of Eden breathed—
   Say, where is she, the beauteous one?

Beneath yon willow's drooping shade,
   With eyes now dim, and lips all pale,
She sleeps in peace. Read on her urn,
   *"A broken heart."* This tells her tale.

And where is he—that tower of strength—
   Whose fate with hers, for life was joined?
How beats his heart, once honor's throne?
   How high has soared his daring mind?

Go to the dungeon's gloom tonight—
   His wasted form, his aching head,
And all that now remains of him,
   Lies, shuddering, on a felon's bed.

Ask you of all these woes the cause?
   The festal board, the enticing bowl

More often came, and reason fled,
  And maddened passions spurned control.

Learn wisdom then. The frequent feast
  Avoid; for there, with stealthy tread
Temptation walks, to lure you on,
  Till death, at last, the banquet spread.

And shun, oh! shun the enchanted cup.
  Though, now, its draught like joy appears,
Ere long, it will be fanned by sighs,
  And sadly mixed with blood and tears.

QUESTIONS — 1. What is meant by "festal board"? 2. What
became of two of the young people who gathered around "the
festal board"? 3. In many of the lessons included in the
READERS, McGuffey wanted to teach that what you do in
your youth affects your adult life. In this poem what is the chief
villain that youth should shun?

SPELL AND DEFINE — (1) garlanded; (3) devoted; (4) enhance; (5) gloriously; (6) sundered; (7) maniac; (8) roseate;
(12) passions.

# LESSON LIV (54)

## *Consequences of Bad Spelling*
### LOND. GIFT.

RULE—In reading humorous pieces, such as excite laughter and merriment, the reader must not laugh at all. He should read to make others laugh, but not laugh himself. If those who listen, laugh so much as to prevent their hearing, the reader may pause until they suspend their laughter and then proceed.

LETTER I — *Miss Emma Walford to her Aunt.*

MY DEAR AUNT: — I take the opportunity of sending a letter by Mr. Green to let you see whether I am improved in my writing, as I wrote to you about this time last year; and to tell you, that I hope you will come to see us soon, as I have so many things to show you. I have been to see a real play since I saw you. I never laughed so much in all my life. It was so curious to see so many people all in tears one above another!

Mr. Bedford comes to see us very often. You know what a droll man he is. He has got a new tail— I am sure you would laugh at it. As the weather is so fine, Mamma allows me to have a great deal of thyme in my garden, which, you know, is very nice. You will be sorry to hear that the old ewe is dead, as it was a great favorite of yours, and all our furs have been destroyed by lightning.

William's paths are all spoiled again, but he has such a bad gait; it always will be so till he can mend it. It is so long since we have seen our cousins that we are afraid they are ill. Papa means to send George tomorrow to sea. It is so warm that I am writing out of doors, close by the beach, with a large plain before me. George has just got a nice plaice, as well as myself. I am very bizzy making nets, as we are going to have a sail tomorrow. I wish you were here.

It is my birthday. Papa has brought me down a beau. He says I am now quite old enough to have a beau, as I can be trusted. I am to have my hair dressed today. I have had several presents, and one is the nicest little deer in the world. I long to buy a fine cage for it.

I am very much obliged to you for the globes you were kind enough to promise me. William gave me a small pair, today. He has been learning to shoot with a gun, and he was near laming himself for life, for he stuffed his toe in so tight he could not get it out, and Papa was afraid the gun would burst. George rowed over to Uncle John's, yesterday. He gave him two new oars to bring home, which he gave me for a birthday present. I have put them into my little cedar box in my Indian cabinet.

I found such a pretty vale, lately, on the road between this and St. Albans. I long to show it to you. It is exactly like a French vale.

I think I have told you all the news.

From your affectionate niece,

EMMA WALFORD

P.S. — Mamma desires me to say that although she has not seen my letter, she told me how to spell all the long, hard words. I must leave off. What a trouble these aunts are. I cannot get rid of them.

SPELL AND DEFINE — Find all of the words that are used incorrectly.

LETTER II — *Mrs. Wilson, to her niece.*

MY DEAR NIECE: — Your letter surprised me exceedingly, as it conveyed much information for which I was not in the least prepared. Your being at the *sea-side* will deter me from visiting your mother at present, as I am not able to take so long a journey. And as you are anxious *"to get rid of your aunts"* (which I really believe you had no intention of writing down in your letter), I will not "trouble" you with my company, but will visit your mother when *you* are away.

I do not imagine I should like your garden very much, as I think that *thyme* is very fit for a kitchen garden. I do not remember that I ever admired your old *ewe*; I used to prefer your little lambs. I never knew before that lightning injured *furs*. I thought that moths were their only enemies. I cannot agree with your father that you require a *beau!* Surely your kind brothers, who are older than yourself, can walk out with you and take care of you.

I cannot guess why William should stuff his *toe* into the barrel of his gun. That is more the act of an idiot than of a sensible boy like him. But I am still more puzzled to know how George could *row* all the way to his uncle's, as there is no water within some miles of Otley Park, nor how you can get a pair of *oars* into your little India cabinet.

I shall be glad to see the pretty valley you have discovered, but, as you have never been in France, how do you know it is like a French *vale?* If the Mr. Bedford you mention is my friend, I should certainly laugh at his folly in wearing a *pigtail*, as he is only twenty-five years of age.

I am truly sorry that your father has decided on sending George to *sea*, as his original plan, of sending him to study for the church, seemed so congenial to his mind and character. I am surprised that your mother should think it right to have your *hair* dressed, as your own natural curls are far better than curls made with hot irons. I think that the little *deer* that has been given you would be much happier in your uncle's park than in a cage. It will look like a wild beast at Exeter 'Change.

William must be very clumsy to walk in such a manner as to destroy his own garden walks. I do not approve of visiting theaters. If the play you saw was so affecting as to excite everyone to *tears*, you must have appeared very silly to be laughing all the time. Was not your seat on the *beach* very hot for want of shade? I cannot conceive how you could attempt to write a letter and catch fish at the same time!

I would enjoy a *sail* very much with you, if I were not considered *troublesome*. I hope the boys will catch plenty of fish in your nets. As William has given you a *pair* of globes, I have just sent off those I intended for you to your cousin Caroline, who, I am sure, will be very glad to get them, as she has not even a *small pair.*

Give my love to your good papa and mamma and the boys, and believe me,

Your sincere friend,

ELIZABETH WILSON

# LESSON LV (55)

## *Bad Spelling*—CONTINUED

RULE—It will be remembered that a dash indicates a pause a little longer than a comma, but care must be taken not to let the voice fall.

LETTER III — *Mrs. Walford to Mrs. Wilson*

### THE GLEBE: ST. ALBANS

Emma has been in despair, my dear sister, ever since the receipt of your letter. She begs me as soon as possible to clear up the mistakes which in her extreme ignorance she has committed. In the first place, she is very anxious that I should tell you how much she loves all her *aunts*, and you most of all.

Had you not returned Emma's letter, your answer would have been quite unintelligible. The boys have been excessively amused, and have, to use their own expression, "quizzed her most unmercifully," but at the least hint from me, I know they will desist.

Naturally ambitious, and a little vain, Emma has always considered English spelling as a disagreeable task. There was no praise, no honor, no glory in spelling well. It was a matter of course, and though it was a disgrace to spell ill, it was no merit to spell well.

She now feels the importance of it, and as soon as I see that she is diligent in learning the "long, dull column of spelling," the subject of the unfortunate letter shall be dropped.

She begs me to tell you that when the weather is fine, I allow her a great portion of *time* to work in her garden, that your favorite *yew*-tree is dead, that our *firs* were destroyed in the last storm, that her papa brought her down a *bow* and arrows, that William stuffed too much *tow* into his gun, amid that he *rode* over to Otley Park on his pony and brought back two pretty specimens of copper *ore*, which he kindly gave her to put among her curiosities.

She found a *veil* in the road the other day, which on comparing with mine, she pronounces to be a French *veil*. Mr. Bedford's new *tale* is one he translated from the Italian, in which a man is persuaded he is another person. It is really a very comic story.

George went to *see* his cousins. Their absence was occasioned by their having some friends staying with them. Philip Ainsworth sent us a *hare*—as it was near Emma's birthday. He begged it might be a present to her. Emma's "little *deer*" is a canary—all her pets are *dear* in her eyes. She thought she had a nice *place* under the *beech* on a bank, but as she was troubled with the *ants*, she was obliged to leave it. She has been making nets to cover pictures for a *sale* in the neighborhood, for some charity.

Her loss of the globes is a great disappointment. Her present from William was a little ivory *pear*, containing seven others, and in the last, a small set of tea-things—an ingenious toy. She was much entertained at the theater and was astonished at the *tiers* of heads in the pit and boxes, as she had never before seen so many people assembled.

Now you find that we are at home, I hope you will not delay coming to give Emma the kiss of reconciliation and the pleasure of your company to

Your affectionate sister,

EMILY WALFORD

P.S. — A partial mother finds excuse for her children when no other person can. Although Emma was eight years old on Thursday, you know how much her delicate health has interfered with her studies.

QUESTIONS — 1. Why did Emma's mother write to Mrs. Wilson? 2. What reason did Emma's mother suggest as the cause of Emma's not learning how to spell? Do young girls use this excuse today? 3. Why is the habit of accurate spelling important to you?

SPELL AND DEFINE — (1) receipt; (2) unintelligible, excessively, quizzed; (3) ambitious; (5) curiosities; (8) astonished.

# LESSON LVI (56)

## *Awake, Zion!*—ISAIAH LII

RULE—This lesson should be read as poetry. Some of the sublimest strains of poetry are from Isaiah's pen. This piece has been arranged so as to exhibit its poetic beauty in greater perfection than in the common translation.

1. Awake! awake! put on thy strength, O Zion!
   Put on thy beautiful garments, O Jerusalem,
      the holy city!
   For henceforth there shall no more
      come into thee
   The uncircumcised and the unclean.

2. Shake thyself from the dust;
   Arise, and sit down, O Jerusalem!
   Loose thyself from the bands of thy neck,
   O captive daughter of Zion!

3. For thus saith the Lord,
   Ye have sold yourselves for nought;
   And ye shall be redeemed without money.

4. For thus saith the Lord God,
   My people went down aforetime into Egypt
     to sojourn there,
   And the Assyrian oppressed them
     without cause.

5. Now therefore, what have I here,
     saith the Lord,
   That my people is taken away for nought?
   They that rule over them make them to howl,
     saith the Lord,
   And my name continually every day is
     blasphemed.

6. Therefore my people shall know my name.
   Therefore they shall know in that day
     that I am he that doth speak:
   Behold! it is I.

7. How beautiful upon the mountains
   Are the feet of him that bringeth good
     tidings—that publisheth peace!
   That bringeth good tidings of good—
     that publisheth salvation!
   That saith unto Zion, Thy God reigneth!

8. The watchmen
   Shall lift up the voice, with the voice together
     shall they sing:
   For they shall see eye to eye,
   When the Lord shall bring again Zion.

9. Break forth into joy, sing together

Ye waste places of Jerusalem!
For the Lord hath comforted his people,
He hath redeemed Jerusalem.

10. The Lord hath made bare his holy arm
In the eyes of all the nations;
And all the ends of the earth
Shall see the salvation of our God.

11. Depart ye! depart ye! go ye out from thence,
Touch no unclean thing;
Go ye out of the midst of her;
Be ye clean, that bear the vessels of the Lord.

12. For ye shall not go out with haste,
Nor go by flight:
For the Lord will go before you;
And the God of Israel shall be your rereward.

# LESSON LVII (57)

## *Ministers of Religion*

RULE—Read this piece with particular care. Any piece that is
worth reading, is worth reading with care.

How beauteous are their feet
  Who stand on Zion's hill;
Who bring salvation on their tongues,
  And words of peace reveal!

How charming is their voice,
  How sweet the tidings are!
Zion! behold thy Savior King,
  "He reigns and triumphs here."

How happy are our ears
  That hear this joyful sound,
Which kings and prophets waited for,
  And sought, but never found!

How blessed are our eyes,
  That see this heavenly light;
Prophets and kings desir'd it long,
  But died without the sight.

The watchmen join their voice,
  And tuneful notes employ;
Jerusalem breaks forth in songs,
  And deserts learn the joy.

The Lord makes bare his arm
  Through all the earth abroad;
Let every nation now behold
  Their Savior and their God.

QUESTIONS — This poem is based on Isaiah LII, the subject of the lesson that immediately precedes this one. 1. Find at least two sentences in Isaiah 52 that are used in this poem. 2. Read Isaiah 52 and "Ministers of Religion" aloud. Compare and contrast the impact or power of each one.

# LESSON LVIII (58)

## *The Destruction of Sennacherib*
### BYRON

RULE—We should read poetry with the same tone, the same
accent and emphasis, and the same regard to pauses that we use
in prose. If the composition is truly poetic, it will appear so
when it is read plainly and without any effort of the reader to
measure it out and make it sound like poetry. If it is not truly
poetic, it is not the reader's duty to make it so.

The Assyrian came down like the wolf on the fold,
And his cohorts were gleaming
    with purple and gold;
And the sheen of their spears
    was like stars on the sea,
When the blue waves roll nightly on deep Galilee.

Like the leaves of the forest
    when summer is green,
That host with their banners at sunset was seen;
Like the leaves of the forest
    when autumn hath blown,
That host on the morrow lay withered and strown.

For the Angel of Death
    spread his wings on the blast,
And breathed in the face of the foe as he passed;
And the eyes of the sleepers
    waxed deadly and chill,
And their hearts but once heaved,
    and forever were still.

And there lay the steed with his nostrils all wide,
But thro' them there rolled
    not the breath of his pride,

And the foam of his gasping lay white on the turf,
And cold as the spray of the rock-beating surf.

And there lay the rider distorted and pale,
With the dew on his brow,
   and the rust on his mail;
And the tents were all silent the banners alone,
The lances unlifted, the trumpet unblown.

And the widows of Ashur are loud in their wail;
And the idols are broke in the temple of Baal;
And the might of the Gentile,
   unsmote by the sword,
Hath melted like snow in the glance of the Lord!

QUESTIONS — 1. Byron based this poem on II Kings 19. Read the Biblical account and explain why Sennacherib's challenge to Israel was really a challenge to Israel's God. 2. In the Biblical account and in the poem, how was the victory over Sennacherib accomplished? 3. The famous last two lines of this poem explain how the foes of the righteous are conquered. In your own words tell how they are conquered.

# LESSON LIX (59)

## On Prayer—LITERARY JOURNAL

RULE—Read this piece with reference to the preceding rules.

Go, when the morning shineth,
  Go, when the moon is bright,
Go, when the eve declineth,
  Go, in the hush of night;
Go with pure mind and feeling,
  Fling earthly thoughts away,

And in thy chamber kneeling,
  Do thou in secret pray.

Remember all who love thee,
  All who are loved by thee;
Pray for those who hate thee,
  If any such there be;
Then for thyself in meekness,
  A blessing humbly claim,
And link with each petition
  Thy great Redeemer's name.

Or if 'tis e'er denied thee
  In solitude to pray,
Should holy thoughts come o'er thee,
  When friends are round thy way,
E'en then the silent breathing
  Of thy spirit raised above,
Will reach His throne of glory,
  Who is Mercy, Truth, and Love.

Oh! not a joy or blessing,
  With this can we compare,
The power that He hath given us
  To pour our souls in prayer.
Whene'er thou pin'st in sadness,
  Before His footstool fall,
And remember in thy gladness,
  His grace who gave thee all.

QUESTIONS — 1. According to the poet, when are appropriate times to pray? 2. For whom should we pray?

# LESSON LX (60)

## *The Dying Boy*—MRS. SIGOURNEY

RULE—In solemn pieces of this kind, you should read slower and more softly than usual.

It must be sweet in childhood, to give back
The spirit to its Maker, ere the heart
Has grown familiar with the paths of sin,
And sown—to garner up its bitter fruits.
I knew a boy whose infant feet had trod
Upon the blossoms of some seven springs,
And when the eighth came round,
      and called him out
To revel in its light, he turned away,
And sought his chamber, to lie down and die.

'Twas night: he summoned his
      accustomed friends,
And on this wise bestowed his last bequest.
  "Mother—I'm dying now!
There's a deep suffocation in my breast,
As if some heavy hand my bosom pressed,—
  And on my brow
  I feel the cold sweat stand;
My lips grow dry and tremulous, and my breath
Comes feebly on. Oh! tell me, is this death?

  Mother, your hand—
  Here—lay it on my wrist,
And place the other thus beneath my head,
And say, sweet Mother, say, when I am dead,
  Shall I be missed?
  Never beside your knee,
Shall I kneel down again at night to pray;

Nor with the morning wake, and sing the lay
  You taught me?
  Oh, at the time of prayer,
When you look round, and see a vacant seat,
You will not wait then for my coming feet—
  You'll miss me there.

  Father, I'm going home!
To the good home you spoke of, that blest land,
Where it is one bright summer always, and
  Storms do never come.
  I must be happy then.
From pain and death you say I shall be free,
That sickness never enters there, and we
  Shall meet again:

  Brother—the little spot
I used to call my garden, where long hours
We've stayed to watch the budding things,
    and flowers,
  Forget it not!
  Plant there some box or pine,
Something that lives in winter, and will be
A verdant offering to my memory,
  And call it mine!

  Sister—my young rose tree,
That all the spring has been my pleasant care,
Just putting forth its leaves so green and fair,
  I give to thee:
  And when its roses bloom,
I shall be far away, my short life done;
But will you not bestow a single one
  Upon my tomb?

  Now, Mother, sing the tune
You sang last night; I'm weary, and must sleep.

Who was it called my name? Nay, do not weep,
  You'll all come soon!"

Morning spread over earth her rosy wings.
And that meek sufferer, cold and ivory pale,
Lay on his couch asleep. The gentle air
Came through the open window, freighted with
The savory odors of the early spring—
He breathed it not; the laugh of passersby
Jarred like a discord in some mournful tune,
But wak'ned not his slumber. He was dead.

QUESTIONS — 1. How old is the dying boy? 2. To which family members does he speak directly? 3. What is the boy's biggest concern as he speaks to each family member? 4. Why is this poem so sad?

SPELL AND DEFINE — (1) chamber; (2) suffocation, tremulous; (3) kneel, vacant; (5) budding; (8) savory.